Communication for t
Early Years

Speech, language, and communication are key to young children's well-being and development. At a time when communication contexts and modalities are becoming increasingly complex and multifaceted, this key text considers how pedagogical approaches, environments, and interactions can be used to develop and harness the voice of the child in the early years.

Communication for the Early Years takes a broad, ecological systems approach to communication to present theoretical approaches and principles which map a child's communication experiences in the home, the early years setting, in the local community, through play, and engagement with digital media and the enabling environment, including the outdoor environment. Topics considered include:

- the role played by pedagogical leadership in the development of an effective communication environment
- aspects of the physical environment which encourage or inhibit communication
- effective communication in and between settings
- the importance of toys and resources
- developments in digital communication and their impact on the child

Chapters consider perspectives of the child, family, and practitioner to encourage a holistic and collaborative understanding of interaction and the role this plays in a child's development, while case studies, examples from practice and reflective questions inspire discussion, challenge thinking, and encourage the application of research in practice.

An in-depth exploration of the factors which impact on the development of a child's communication skills, this will be key reading for students and practitioners in the Early Years, as well as those involved in their training and continued professional development.

Julie Kent is Senior Lecturer and Course Leader of the BA (Hons) Childhood Studies Degree at Nottingham Trent University, UK.

Moira Moran was formerly Senior Lecturer on the EYITT PGCE, as well as on the BA (Hons) Childhood Studies Degree at Nottingham Trent University, UK.

Communication for the Early Years

A Holistic Approach

Edited by Julie Kent and Moira Moran

Routledge
Taylor & Francis Group

LONDON AND NEW YORK

First published 2019
by Routledge
2 Park Square, Milton Park, Abingdon, Oxon OX14 4RN

and by Routledge
52 Vanderbilt Avenue, New York, NY 10017

Routledge is an imprint of the Taylor & Francis Group, an informa business

British Library Cataloguing-in-Publication Data
A catalogue record for this book is available from the British Library

Library of Congress Cataloging-in-Publication Data
Names: Kent, Julie Ruth, 1965- editor. | Moran, Moira, editor.
Title: Communication for the early years: a holistic approach/
edited by Julie Kent and Moira Moran.
Description: Abingdon, Oxon; New York, NY: Routledge, 2019. |
Includes bibliographical references and index.
Identifiers: LCCN 2018054361 (print) | LCCN 2019013475 (ebook) |
ISBN 9781351166447 (eb) | ISBN 9780815348603 (hb: alk. paper) |
ISBN 9780815348610 (pb: alk. paper) | ISBN 9781351166447 (ebook)
Subjects: LCSH: Early childhood education. | Interpersonal
communication–Study and teaching (Early childhood) |
Communication in education. | Children–Language. |
Child development.
Classification: LCC LB1139.23 (ebook) | LCC LB1139.23 .C64 2019 (print) |
DDC 372.21–dc23
LC record available at https://lccn.loc.gov/2018054361

ISBN: 978-0-8153-4860-3 (hbk)
ISBN: 978-0-8153-4861-0 (pbk)
ISBN: 978-1-351-16644-7 (ebk)

Typeset in Melior
by Deanta Global Publishing Services, Chennai, India
Printed by CPI Group (UK) Ltd, Croydon CR0 4YY

We dedicate this book to all those colleagues, students, practitioners, families, and, most importantly, children who we have worked with throughout our careers. We value the learning experiences they have provided us with along the way and acknowledge and thank them for the rich contribution they have made to the writing of our chapters.

Contents

Preface

Fundamental to the well-being of children is their communication experience. Roberts (2010) in her ABC model of well-being identifies the centrality of communication and the need for "companionable learning where well-being develops". Communication is how children explore their world and, as practitioners and teachers, the understanding of the bi-directional relationship between the child and the contexts or systems that surround them is a theoretical perspective which supports the way that we work with children and seek to develop pedagogical approaches to enhance children's learning and development in this area (Bronfenbrenner 1998). In the Early Years Foundation Stage (EYFS) (Dept for Education, Great Britain 2017), communication and language are among the prime areas of learning and development and, in the ecological systems theoretical model, communication sits as central to the development of the child.

There is a growing body of research in the area of child well-being and there is also a growing sense that the communication environment is in no small way connected to the well-being of the child (Manning-Morton 2014). Recent Ofsted reports (2015 and 2016) have highlighted the need for prioritisation of speech, language, and communication as a "cornerstone of leaders' work" with disadvantaged children, especially funded two-year-olds, and have noted that "around one quarter of disadvantaged children were unable to communicate effectively because they lacked the concentration, vocabulary and listening skills to focus their attention and understand what others were saying".

This book considers the communication contexts around the child, from an ecological systems view from the micro-system in the home setting, through the meso-system and exo-system of culture and community, the macro-system of educational and public health policy, and through global influences on the individual child at the centre. In particular the changing nature of the medium of communication will be explored in relation to children's digital experiences.

The book will bring together research from a range of sources to support the teaching of future and current Early Years (EY) practitioners, to develop their application of research to combine academic and practice-based perspectives to inform practice.

Each chapter will contain case study examples and evidence from current research projects and will provide reflective questions to support discussion in taught sessions for continuing professional development and will provide challenges to thinking about practice based on a holistic understanding of the communication contexts for the child.

Julie Kent and Moira Moran

About the contributors

Helen Cazaly

Helen Cazaly is a Senior Lecturer at Nottingham Trent University delivering on the Childhood Studies BA (Hons) programme. She is also a Trustee at the Professional Association for Childcare and Early Years (PACEY) which acts as an important advocate for the Early Years sector. Her professional background includes being an owner/manager of an Early Years setting as well as teaching childhood and education for BTEC and CACHE students in FE colleges. Helen was also very involved in the Mentoring programme for the original Early Years Professional Status for both the Open University/National Day Nurseries partnership as well as for South West Initiative for Training.

Caroline Farley

Caroline Farley has worked in children's services for over 25 years in leadership roles within private, charitable, and local authority settings, and is presently Head of Nursery at Loughborough University. As an independent early childhood consultant she has been commissioned by several local authorities in the East Midlands to review services and pilot projects and deliver training and development. Caroline is dedicated to promoting excellent practice and has shared her expertise and knowledge at local, national, and regional conferences and events. Her current research is pedagogical leadership.

Catherine Gripton

Dr Catherine Gripton is an experienced lecturer, author, and researcher. She is an Assistant Professor in the School of Education at the University of Nottingham and has a special interest in 3–7 education, early childhood mathematics, and children's experiences of school. Catherine was a teacher in Nottingham and Nottinghamshire primary schools for 14 years, teaching nursery and infant classes and becoming an advanced skills teacher for Early Years in 2003. Catherine is part of the primary education team at the University of Nottingham.

Sue Hobson

Sue Hobson is an Early Years Consultant. She is an experienced Early Years teacher who has worked in the East End of London and in Leicester and Leicestershire.

She worked for over 12 years with Leicester City's Early Years Support Team as a peripatetic teacher of children from birth to five who have additional needs. In that role she worked closely with children's families, other professionals, and practitioners in nurseries and schools.

She has a particular interest in special needs, English as an additional language, family learning, and the impact attachment has on the behaviour and emotional well-being of our youngest children. She is an enthusiastic and creative trainer who enjoys the challenge of making learning accessible and enjoyable to a varied audience.

Sue is a mother of five and grandmother of eight and lives in Leicester with her husband, Pete.

Julie Kent

Julie Kent is a Senior Lecturer and Course Leader on the Childhood Studies BA (Hons) programme at Nottingham Trent University. Her current research is in the communication environment in EY settings and she works closely with the SLT team in the county in this area. Prior to working in Higher Education, Julie led the team in a Sure Start Children's Centre in rural Northamptonshire with a focus on developing the inter-agency working and the early communication support for children and families. She is also a qualified Speech and Language Therapist, having worked in the NHS with children in school and community settings for 15 years. She is a Makaton Regional Tutor.

Sarah McDonald

Sarah McDonald is a Clinical Psychologist and Lecturer in Psychology at Nottingham Trent University. In terms of childhood development, she is interested in how new interventions that have been shown to be effective theoretically or in research settings can be implemented effectively in real-world environments.

Moira Moran

Moira Moran taught in and led teams in Nursery units and schools for more than 20 years, first in London then in Nottingham. She subsequently joined a team of local Authority Early Years Specialist Teachers supporting the PVI sector and teachers in Foundation units. As a Lecturer and Course Leader at Nottingham Trent University, she developed outdoor learning and Forest School approaches with students, practitioners, and children.

Sheine Peart

Dr Sheine Peart has worked in education for over 30 years in schools, colleges, local authorities, further education, higher education, and youth and community settings. She has taught numeracy, communication, and science to students on vocational programmes and was the manager of teacher education courses in further education (FE). She has been an equalities manager and previously led a team dedicated to raising the achievement of African Caribbean pupils. She is currently the manager of the NASENCO programme at Nottingham Trent University and previously managed the PhD Education programme. She continues to contribute to Masters in Education and undergraduate courses.

Carole Ulanowsky

Children's issues have been at the forefront of Dr Ulanowsky's 30 years' teaching and research in Higher Education from a range of perspectives – psychological, educational, sociological, and philosophical. Her work as Trustee/Director of the charity 'What about the Children?' focuses on children's emotional well-being and their positioning in society and how current trends and values impact on early care/educational environments, for better or worse.

Dr Ulanowsky was awarded a PhD from the Open University in 2008 for her intergenerational study of women's perceptions of motherhood. She is currently working on a new series: "I wish I'd known about... MAGIC BABIES/MAGIC CHILDREN/MAGIC TEENAGERS".

Dr Ulanowsky has four children and six grandchildren.

Introduction

A theoretical and ideological basis for the discussion of communication in the early years

Julie Kent

The communication context of children's worlds is constantly changing and has probably never been more complex and multifaceted. Conversely, access to a vast range of modalities for communication has never been easier or more widely available. This book is aimed as a resource for early years educators and also teachers and tutors who work with students engaged in a range of study in early years and childhood. There are a number of theoretical approaches and principles, developmental, cultural, and organisational, which can be applied to children's communication environments in their early years. A key question which this book hopes to explore is whether and how our "communication-rich" environments correlate with the provision and experience of a "language-rich" environment for the child where their own communication and development is enhanced and where the messages which they receive about themselves and the communication that we engage in about them is affirming and enhances their learning and development. The concept of child voice and how it is nurtured, listened to, and understood in the context of early years settings and the earliest communication relationships is fundamental to developing a holistic perspective on children's communication in the early years and central to the author's understanding throughout the text.

The ecological context

Bronfenbrenner (2004) proposed an ecological systems view of the environments in which human development occurs. If a child's development is seen as a series of ecological transitions that encompass the child's whole reality it is possible to demonstrate the centrality of communication in each of these systems, from the most personal and intimate early relationships in the home, through early educational experiences and community encounters to the impact of culture, policy, education, and society's view. Although each individual has their own developmental trajectory, Bronfenbrenner's socio-cultural theory states that human development occurs as the individual actively engages with the social environment that they live in, within the time period they exist in, and nowhere is this seen more clearly than in relation to the communication environment. The early years practitioner has a central role as a mediator in managing and supporting communication between the child's systems.

Communication beyond the curriculum

Thus the book aims to move beyond the Early Years Foundation Stage (EYFS) understanding of Communication and Language as one area of learning and development, albeit a prime area, to engage with the wider understanding of communication as a social justice concern and a key to children's well-being (Brebner et al. 2016). Recent research findings demonstrate that their communication experience is fundamental to the well-being of children (Law et al. 2017). Roberts (2011) in her research, which was underpinned by her theoretical ABC model of well-being, identifies the centrality of communication in developing and supporting a child's well-being and highlights the need for "companionable learning ... whereby well-being develops" (p 33). Her research focuses on the micro-level of the child's environment and the reciprocal dialogue between the child and their earliest companions, whether these are parents, carers, siblings, or peers. This view is grounded in social constructivist theoretical perspectives of Vygotsky (1978) and the attachment theories of Bowlby (1997) and is explored in relation to children's communication, through theory, research, and practice in Ulanowsky's initial chapter as she examines the developmental and current social context of a child's early communication relationships and language learning opportunities.

> *Bruner came to view language development as a collaborative outcome of the curiosity of a highly sociable infant, engaged with loquacious story-making companions intent upon ritualizing and symbolizing the game of life.*
>
> (Bruner in Trevarthen 2015 p 39)

Practitioners, depending on when, where, and in what field they have studied, will have a varying view of children's communication and how it develops. Some traditions support an understanding from the mechanistic view developed by Chomsky of the Language Acquisition Device, whereas others may hold a view which recognises the central role of individual cognitive development through pre-defined stages espoused by Piaget. This is particularly evident in current approaches which highlight the schematic nature of children's learning through repeated behaviours and "questions" that children ask of the environment through their behaviour and activity. Many may have a social constructivist viewpoint, based on Vygotsky's theoretical perspective of the communication system as a tool for learning and thinking which develops in the context of relationships and the modelling of the more knowledgeable other. This view, along with Bruner's concept of the scaffolding of the knowledgeable practitioner, underpins many current approaches to early years education, particularly the EYFS where the adult role in positive relationships and providing the enabling environment is seen as central to the child's learning and development. Many more may have embraced a more holistic view which encompasses a range and combination of all of the above.

The communication relationship

Alongside Robert's (2010) concepts of "agency" and a sense of "belonging", communication is described as a process of connection, echoing the bi-directional relationship identified by Bronfenbrenner, which underpins the child's relationships and sense of self within these relationships. Roberts (ibid.) clearly emphasises the relational nature of communication, not only the vocabulary and "talk" that the child is exposed to. Children explore their world through the medium of communication and, as practitioners and teachers, the understanding of the bi-directional relationship between the child and the contexts or systems that surround them is a theoretical perspective which supports the way that professionals work with children and seek to develop pedagogical approaches to enhance children's learning and development in this area (Bronfenbrenner 2004). In the EYFS, Communication and Language is one of the prime areas of learning and development and, in the ecological systems theoretical model, communication sits as central to the development of the child.

There are resonances here with the social pedagogical approach to working with children where the practitioner "sees (themselves) as a person, in relationship with the child" (Cameron and Moss 2011 p 9). Relationship and communication are central themes within social pedagogical practice and has echoes in the holistic view of the "whole child" which is strong in good early years practice. Social pedagogues value the whole community as well as the educational setting, as being central to providing an environment where the child's well-being and learning is developed (ibid.). Gripton, in her chapter on communicating children's perspectives, takes the position of a social pedagogue as she considers the child as an active participant in wider society, emphasising the centrality of listening to the child's voice and challenging practitioners to really consider how they might reach a full and open understanding of what this might be and how it might be heard.

Communication and long-term outcomes

A significant image within this pedagogical approach is the diamond model of the individual (Holthoff and Eichsteller 2009 in Cameron and Moss 2011) with one of its key facets of well-being and happiness having a basis in positive experiences throughout the lifespan. Clearly this foundation of positive experiences begins in the early years, moving from the initial home relationships, into the setting and the wider community. It is likely that the setting itself will be a reflection of the community in which it is situated and this is of relevance, particularly in areas of social disadvantage. Bronfenbrenner would suggest that communication is about identity formation and will situate the individual within a community through the communication relationships which take place.There is an increasing body of research in the area of child well-being and there is also a growing sense across disciplines that supports the view that the communication environment is in no small way connected to the well-being of the child (Manning-Morton 2014). Recent Ofsted reports (2015 and 2016) have highlighted the need for prioritisation of speech, language, and communication as a "cornerstone of leaders' work" with disadvantaged children, especially funded two-year-olds and have noted that "around one quarter of disadvantaged children were unable to communicate effectively because they lacked the concentration, vocabulary and listening skills to focus their attention and understand what others were saying" (p 16).

It is impossible to escape the fact that disadvantage and associated delays in early language acquisition are significant predictors of achievement, well beyond the early years (Law et al. 2017) and it is noteworthy that previous research has also suggested that early years practitioners have had low levels of confidence and skills in the area of identifying children's communication difficulties (Mroz and Hall 2003; Farley et al. 2016). Hobson and Farley in their chapter take a wide view of the communication experiences of children in an early years provision. They reflect on the learning of staff based on their research into the learning journey that challenged and supported the setting staff team to develop their own communication skills and consequently their own confidence and skills in creating a language-rich environment in which children's holistic communication was prioritised and communication between staff in the setting enabled the establishment and ongoing development of the setting communication environment . This chapter identifies the pedagogical leadership approaches that support the needs of learners in the implementation and embedding of a setting-wide communication project into practice and reflects on how learning in the adults within the setting led to a community of practice with an improved communication environment for staff and children alike.

As previously noted, Trevarthen (2015) in his studies makes a link between communication and child mental health, and current research in the area of baby brain development now provides a strong neurological context which supports the understanding of the role of attachment in sharing meaning and understanding (Ulanowsky and Periera-Gray 2015). His concept of intersubjectivity is an essential one for anyone involved in creating, supporting, or engaging in the child's earliest experiences. The concept of attachment (Bowlby 1991) fits well with Bronfenbrenner's ecological systems theory which emphasises the interconnectedness between the child and their environment, the most significant of which is the immediate microsystem formed by the earliest and closest relationships in the child's world and experience. Early years practitioners are in the position of not only needing to understand the child's microsystem but also to recognise that they are a key part of the child's communication world.

The influence of ideological views of communication

The ecological systems approach to a child's learning and development provides a framework for understanding that, as well as theoretical influences on the practitioner's understanding of communication, the early years is also a field within which professional and cultural ideology and policy decisions are played out with significant consequences for the child at the centre. Early years practitioners may be caught up in trying to deliver the best care and education that they can, based on their own knowledge and skills and understanding of theory in practice within the constraints of a wider political agenda which does not always culminate in the best outcomes for the child. Returning to the previously mentioned Ofsted reports, which clearly identify the significance of the implications for children in the early years with poor communication skills in terms of their educational outcomes, there is no doubting the level of concern and the recognition of the need to take action in this area. However, the response to this can be not to return to theoretical principles but to take a pragmatic and policy driven approach to provide for these children more formalised learning and teaching in the areas of language, in particular literacy, rather than considering the underpinning relational elements within the child's microsystem where the wider picture of communication in all its forms could be addressed. Although there is a clear link between children's literacy development and their language skills (Roulstone 2011), the discussion so far would suggest that these skills cannot easily be taught without the rich and stimulating environment which is provided within reciprocal communication relationships. Practitioners within the early years may find themselves at the centre of balancing the needs of the child within the microsystem against the demands of policy from the macrosystem which may confuse, contradict, and even at times work against what good practice is being implemented. Of more note is that it is extremely likely that they are not aware that this is in fact the case.

To give an example, the decision to offer free childcare to disadvantaged two-year-olds is based on the evidence about the lower achievement of these children from disadvantaged backgrounds (Law et al. 2017) and setting staff may be aware of the imperative to support these most vulnerable children. However, in reality, the additional cost for resourcing which these children place on settings may make it difficult for the setting to provide the education and care required, particularly in the climate of the reduction of LA specialist support teams. Nowhere is this dilemma more evident than in relation to communication and children with Speech, Language and Communication Needs (SLCN). In its 2018 report, The Communication Trust emphasises the connections between a child's communication and language and their life chances, and draws attention to the research which identifies competence in this area as a protective factor for the developing child, with good communication in the early years laying the foundation for well-being, resilience, and good mental health in later life. Although SLCN are present in children from across the social spectrum, their prevalence is known to be higher in children from areas of socio-economic disadvantage (Law et al. 2017).

In relation to the wider cultural and policy context it is also relevant to note that communication and language, not just as a learning and development concern but also as a public health issue, is rising up the agenda educationally and politically. Research into the communication environment and the knowledge and skills of early years practitioners suggests a significant degree of variation in the quality of the communication environment encountered by children in early years settings. Kent and McDonald in their chapter discuss the findings of their research into an approach to staff development in this area in Nottinghamshire where the Speech and Language Therapy team have worked closely with setting staff to develop the role of the Language Lead within settings across the county as part of a commissioned universal service in response to the communication needs of children as a public health issue. The chapter will present an understanding of good practice in the current context, examining enablers and barriers to collaborative working and considering the centrality of leadership of learning in this area. It will reflect on what the research findings suggest for the wider public health agenda, bringing it back to the practitioner and the child's learning environment at the centre.

Right at the start of the statutory guidance for the implementation of the EYFS it is acknowledged that "a child's experiences between birth and age five have a major impact on their future life chances" (DfE 2017 p 5) and consequently, in the early years setting, practitioners are responsible for routinely observing and tracking children's learning and development across the prime and specific areas. It is made clear that educational programmes, of whatever nature, must provide a "language-rich environment" and communication and language is one of "three areas (which) are particularly crucial for igniting children's curiosity and enthusiasm for learning, and for building their capacity to learn, form relationships and thrive" (DfE 2017 p 7).

The concept of "thriving" embraces deep aspects of survival, growth, and the capacity to flourish, and, from an ecological systems perspective, encompasses the interaction between the child and their environment. Gripton, in her chapter about the communication environment, considers the EYFS theme of the enabling environment and reflects on the environment as a shared learning space where ideas are co-constructed and communication relationships are mediated between practitioners and children. She challenges practitioners to consider how the environment can be both a facilitator and a barrier to communication and examines the responsibilities of adults in promoting communication in all its forms. Moran's chapter on the outdoor enabling environment further applies theoretical and practice models to the understanding of how the outdoor environment acts as a powerful medium through which new, different, and surprising communication relationships can be established to engender confidence and voice in children who may not have flourished so well in other more formal classroom environments. Practitioners in the early years will need to consider what this has to say in relation not only to the provision in the setting but also to the relationships between the elements within the child's microsystem, the mesosystem. Does what happens in the early years stay in the early years or are there implications for practice beyond the early years microsystem? It is evident that there are multiple connections between theoretical perspectives and that these must be viewed in the widest of contexts which include the educational, cultural, and family spheres as well as community, policy, and statutory domains. In these contexts, the ecological systems perspective supports practitioners to understand the way in which the systems around the child operate and the centrality of their role in mediating practice, implementing policy and working with communities to support communication within, with, and about the child in their early years experiences.

The changing communication context

In relation to the child's cultural environment, or, Bronfenbrenner's macrosystem, it is essential that within the early years we recognise what experiences, knowledge, and understanding children already bring to the setting and much of this will be linked to their family lifestyles, community, and culture. The way in which early years practitioners represent those lifestyles and communities in the setting will communicate a great deal to the child about how their culture is viewed and valued. Therefore a key aspect of the enabling environment is the consistent representation of the worlds of the children within it. Practitioners will need to consider the bi-directional nature of these environmental communications which may include the materials, resources, and representations of communities within the setting as well as the language used or not used by practitioners with children. Peart, in her chapter on children's images reflected through toys, examines the messages that are communicated to children by misrepresentation or omission of their own world and culture in the resources which are provided within an early years setting and challenges practitioners to consider the responsibilities of the setting in this area in representing the diverse nature of children and childhoods in the materials offered in a setting.

In the widest possible aspects of our society it is also evident that the nature of communication is changing and this is affecting not only professional practice but also parenting and the connections between parents and professionals. In Cazaly's chapter on the role of digital media in communication systems in early years practice, she reflects on how the minute details of the child's microsystem and daily world can be instantly and permanently thrown into the widest possible arena well beyond their own lives through social media, and discusses the responsibilities of practitioners in a policy and rights-based framework in negotiating this fraught area in how they respond to the new global context of communication and the documentation of children's lives within it, as well as supporting parents to understand this area and their involvement in the child's mesosystem.

Finally, this book considers the communication contexts around the child, from an ecological systems view from the microsystem in home and setting, through the mesosystem and exosystem of culture and community and the macrosystem of policy and global influences on the individual child at the centre. It is hoped that in its broad and eclectic approach to communication, this book will bring together research from a range of sources to support the teaching of future and current early years practitioners, to develop their application of research to combine academic and practice-based perspectives to inform practice.

Each chapter will contain case study examples and evidence from current research projects and will provide reflective questions to support discussion in taught sessions for continuing professional development and will provide challenges to thinking about practice based on a holistic understanding of the communication contexts for the child.

PROVOCATIONS

▪ How might you support students to consider a child's communication and language beyond the boundaries of the EYFS?

▪ Consider the challenges of providing a language-rich environment which is also focused on the child's well-being.

▪ Are practitioners able to weigh their assessments of a child's communication and language development with what they know about their wider communication environment to plan relevant provisions that have an impact for the child?

▪ How might practitioners consider the wider environment of the child when planning support for children with SLCN?

References

Bowlby, J., 1991. 2nd ed. *Attachment and loss trilogy (Vol 1, attachment).* Harmondsworth: Penguin Books.

Bowlby, J., 1997. *Attachment. Vol. 1 (Attachment and loss).* London: Pimlico.

Brebner, C., Jovanovic, J., Lawless, A., and Young, J., 2016. Early childhood educators' understanding of early communication: Application to their work with young children. *Child Language Teaching and Therapy,* 32 (3), 277–292.

Bronfenbrenner, U., 2004. *The ecology of human development: Experiments by nature and design.* Cambridge, MA: Harvard University Press.

Cameron, C., and Moss, P., 2011. *Social pedagogy and working with children and young people: Where care and education meet.* London: Jessica Kingsley.

Department for Education, 2017. *Statutory framework for the early years foundation stage.* London: Department for Education.

Farley, C., Hobson, S., and Kent, J., 2016. *An evidence-base for organisational change based on pedagogical leadership.* TACTYC conference paper [unpublished].

Holthoff, S., and Eichsteller, G. 2009. Conceptual foundations of social pedagogy: A transnational perspective from Germany. Ch. 2, pp. 33–52 in Cameron etc.

Law, J., Charlton, J., and Asmussen, K., 2017. *Language as a child well-being indicator.* London: Early Intervention Foundation.

Manning-Morton, J., 2014. *Exploring well-being in the early years.* Berkshire: OUP.

Mroz, M., and Hall, E., 2003. Not yet identified: The knowledge, skills and training needs of Early Years professionals in relation to children's speech and language development. *Early Years: An International Journal of Research and Development,* 23 (2), 117–130.

Roberts, R., 2010. *Wellbeing from birth.* London: Sage.

Roberts, R., 2011. Companionable learning: A mechanism for holistic well-being development from birth. *European Early Childhood Education Research Journal,* 19 (2), 195–205.

Roulstone, S., Law, J., Rush, R., Clegg, J., and Peters, T., 2011. *Investigating the role of language in children's early educational outcomes.* DfE Research Report 134.

The Communication Trust, 2018. *Written evidence from The Communication Trust Education Select Committee Life Chances Inquiry.* London: The Communication Trust.

The Office for Standards in Education, Children's Services and Skills, 2015. *Early Years Report.* Manchester: OFSTED.

The Office for Standards in Education, Children's Services and Skills, 2016. *Unknown children: Destined for disadvantage.* Manchester: OFSTED.

Trevarthen, C., 2015. Awareness of infants: What do they, and we, seek? *Psychoanalytic Inquiry*, 35, 395–416.

Ulanowsky, C., and Periera-Gray, D., 2015. *Infant mental health: Factors affecting optimal development. London: Evidence for Enquiry.* All Party Parliamentary Group on Children (The First 1001 Days). Available at: www.whataboutthechildren.org.uk [accessed 20.06.18].

Vygotsky, L.S., 1978. *Mind in society: The development of higher psychological processes.* Cambridge, MA: Harvard University Press.

2 Let's begin at the beginning…

Carole Ulanowsky

OVERVIEW OF CHAPTER

This chapter engages with a dichotomy of opportunity. It explores why, in a communication-rich environment, some children are enabled to be effective communicators: language rich, confident, ready to learn, and socially competent, whilst others are not. The discussion focuses especially on the first 3 years of life, actually the "first 3 and a bit" years, because the infant's first experience of language is in the womb. Through research, theoretical perspectives and debate, children's earliest communication experiences will be examined and the role of the responsive adult and their influence on the child's development during this sensitive period will be considered.

The perinatal period

We may marvel at how children accomplish the complex and sophisticated task of language learning. However, a broader question, posed by philosophers through millennia, asks how children, given their limited experience, come to know as much as they do. Certainly, the infant brain is structurally designed for absorption and understanding, and the earliest environment is critical for establishing the process of communication (Chomsky, 1976).

The mother's voice and her rhythm of life becomes for the unborn child an acoustic and emotional link between pre- and post-birth, and, for the baby, this early exposure acts as a form of tuning into sounds specific to its mother tongue. In the early months of life it is the mother's voice that will most effectively stimulate the learning centres of the infant brain and high-pitched baby-talk, sometimes called *motherese*, will be preferred. Indeed, studies have demonstrated that use of the higher voice pitch in the early weeks lead to a richer vocabulary once speech becomes established.

Research demonstrates that from the earliest moments, it is the mother's voice that will activate the language learning centres of the infant brain. Additionally, it is this "auditory face" that will regulate the child's response to stressful situations by reducing the hormone cortisol and stimulating the bonding chemical oxytocin (Beauchemin et al., 2010; Abrams et al., 2016). Eliens (2016) videoed babies to raise awareness to parents and staff in maternity units of the importance of early communication in "The Golden Hour", the baby's amazing alertness in the first 60 minutes or so after birth. This window of opportunity is ripe for first communicative engagement between parent and child, likewise affording potential for early socio/emotional connections forming the first foundation of their relationship. Indeed, we are reminded that neonates are not "blank slates" but have "brains pre-loaded with software tools" for learning about "people, communication and the world at large" (Dewar, 2018 np). For all that, in a recent survey of 1026 adults aged from 16–64 commissioned by www.whataboutthechildren.org.uk almost half (44%) respondents disagreed with the statement: "From the minute after birth new-born babies are ready and able to communicate". Interestingly, 2/3 of those who agreed with the statement were women, with 40% of men disagreeing, some strongly (www.whataboutthechildren.org.uk, 2018).

Yet it is the case that a facility for social engagement is present from the first hours of life and a baby will recognise, and indeed show a preference for, familiar faces, initially, the mother's. Then, in the early weeks, the baby will follow the parent or carer's gaze. By 6–12 months, gaze-following is a strong predictor of language skills and social competence. In summary, from earliest days, smiling at the baby and talking to her, verbally interpreting, and mirroring her expressions, picking up desire cues and commenting on them, will develop an emotional closeness at the same time as establishing and accelerating communication. Thus, neurological connections are activated in the early weeks and months. However, without appropriate stimulus, these connections will atrophy:

Early experience establishes the formation of major neurological pathways in the infant brain, including the direction and level of intellectual competence, psycho-social and even physical health, life-long.
                                        (Ulanowsky and Pereira-Gray, 2015, p 2)

Recent science suggests significant and far-reaching implications for the early care environment – evidencing a strong correlation between emotional security and cognitive development. But more than that, the foundation of sound mental health and happy socialisation through life requires positive early experience to ensure the child's development of a secure "internal working model" along with a positive and confident world view, with all that this implies. The young child constructs a "mental model" of her or his environment; "Brains will do this in order to make sense of their world, to anticipate it, manage it, and negotiate it" (Howe, 2011, p 33).

Sound Attachment – the foundation of emotional health

One to one engagement between the child and her carers will be critical, for early life is experienced through the lens of the earliest relationships. Sound emotional attachment is part of this because, from earliest days, attachment status will impact on the child's overall development, inner security, resilience, and potential for learning. Whether the infant child is being cared for within the family or in the Baby Room of a nursery, it is important that whoever provides this care understands the attachment process and how it can be sustained from first primary relationship with the mother to secondary attachments within settings. (See later discussion of the Key Person role in settings.)

The baby's biological capacity to form attachments is present at birth. Attachment is a survival instinct which drives the child to maintain close proximity with its key carer. Attachment behaviour is at its most intense between 6 and 24 months. Once attachment is secure and feels reliable the infant will confidently begin to explore the world beyond her safe base: from "fusion" with the mother/key carer, to individuation (Ulanowsky and Pereira-Gray, 2015). Attachment status, forged through these early parent/infant interactions is found to be a critical predictor of a child's development in several ways, including language. Indeed, "attachment" and "communication" are inseparable bedfellows, for a child's urge to communicate, and to be communicated with, is manifest from first hours and days.

To connect and communicate with her baby requires sensitive alertness of the mother to her child's signals of feelings and needs. Critical also must be her acceptance of, and respect for, the baby as an individual which is a pre-requisite for establishing healthy parent/child relations (Pawlby, 2018). Above all, it is important for the child that her parents engage in a process of "mind-mindfulness" or "mentalisation", a facility for holding representations of her baby as a person with a mind of their own. In some ways, the parent/child relationship is symbiotic because, being highly sensitive to mood and tone of voice, the young infant likewise will try to discern the mind of the parent. Bronfenbrenner recognised the bi-directional reality of parent/child relationships being the child's responses and temperament impacting on the parent, just as parenting style and input will impact on the child (Gray and Mac Blain, 2015).

A surge of oestrogen, prolactin, and oxytocin in late pregnancy chemically prepares the mother to care for her young. Her intensity of focus and concern actually generates changes in the size and structure of her own brain, especially to the frontal lobes (Kinsley et al., 2011). Actual visible reduction in brain volume can be observed in mothers who hold negative feelings towards their infants. However, as Mileva-Seitz et al. (2013) remind us, the intensity and nature of maternal response to her child can vary considerably, being dependent on personal factors like genetic make-up and experience of how she herself was mothered.

Thus, it is the parent's own "internal working model" that will influence the quality of early relationships for better, or worse, whether "balanced", "disengaged", or "distorted" (Barlow, 2018; Murray and Cooper, 2018). From detailed studies, these authors reveal how parental mood and mental health status impacts on the early attachment process. The strength of the infant's attachment status will depend upon levels of eye contact, being talked to, sung to, and cuddled. Each element will impact on the child's later capacity to function including verbal communication and capacity to form relationships. Unfortunately, parents suffering emotional or mental health difficulties themselves (especially depression) will be "less likely to engage in practices that scaffold and enrich their child's experiences" (Murray,and Cooper, 2018, p 59) and research would suggest that overall, boys are more adversely affected by their mothers' negative mental states, than are girls.

For a child, any form of maternal rejection or emotional coldness is a barrier to emotional and cognitive functioning in very many ways including, for some children, an inability to self-regulate, causing them to indulge in "externalising behaviour" both at home and in early years settings. In many cases, "inside the child is quietly raging against the parental rejection and is developing high levels of hate" (Baron-Cohen, 2012, p 50). Research suggests that an inability to express deeply felt frustration in infancy can emerge as explosive violence later on. In summary, how we are treated as vulnerable infants can have significant impact on later emotional and mental health, including levels of empathy towards others, not least as parents, later on (Baron-Cohen, 2012).

Child development specialists have observed a link between delayed language understanding and acquisition and emotional or behavioural problems. In Clegg et al.'s 2015 study, behaviour at age 6 was scored for difficulties with emotion, conduct, hyperactivity, and poor interaction with their peers. Overall, there was found to be a significant connection between negative elements of behaviour and lower levels of receptiveness, or understood language especially.

International initiatives

Programmes designed to promote, enhance and deepen parents' and others' emotional connection and communication with young children are now widely available. The Video Interaction Guidance (VIGG) programme, (University of

Leiden, personal communication, 2015), is now disseminated globally and regularly utilised by Health, Education, and Social Care staff. This relationship-based programme uses selected video clips of parent/child interactions, previously recorded, to help parents and others become more attuned and responsive to their children concerning what the little ones are trying to communicate, both verbally and non-verbally.

In the early 1990s, Hart and Ridley's ground-breaking study among American families highlighted some dramatic differences in academic and socio-emotional outcomes for children/young people, as significantly dependent on levels of home vocabulary during infancy. Not least, early opportunities for communication, or lack of these, were shown to impact on later IQ levels (Kuhl, 2011). Overall, research has demonstrated how interaction/interface between genes and environment can influence children's development in profound ways.

With the aim of increasing parent/infant verbal interactions among populations in the United States, certain initiatives have been set in place. For example, Health Specialists operationalised a so-called 'SafeCare' training module, now disseminated in the UK (Guinn et al., 2018). These authors cite the 'Providence Talks' project which supplies parents with a free "pedometer", counting parent/child verbal interactions through each day. Wide differences were found in later measures of 12-year-olds' academic achievement between those who had received significant levels of one to one communication in early infancy, and those who had not. Researchers find that later catch-up is not possible when children present with a range of communication difficulties, often linked to problematic behaviour impacting significantly on their learning, such as an ability to *listen*.

Meanwhile, the 'Roots of Empathy' emotional literacy programme (Social Innovation Generation, n.d.) developed in Canada and now having international reach is delivered to 'pre-parents' in high schools. Arrangements are made for parents of young babies to visit classes at 3-week intervals. On each occasion, the baby's development is observed by the young people who are encouraged by a "Roots of Empathy" trainer to label the baby's feelings and what he/she may be trying to communicate, both verbally and non-verbally. The hope is that, if and when these young people become parents, or perhaps childcare workers, they will remember and be influenced by this experience.

21st century environment

> *The overall development of society in the last 50 years has been inimical to the nurturance of children and we have allowed it to be so.*
>
> (Leach, 2018, p 9)

A recent survey conducted by 780 school leaders, in partnership with the Family and Childcare Trust, recorded a majority of respondents as registering a concern about young children's "school readiness" (Family and Childcare Trust, 2017). A total of 86% were of the opinion this had worsened in the previous 5 years, with communication and physical skills highlighted as of particular concern. The report quotes Goddard Blythe, author and Director of The Institute for Neuro-Physiological Psychology, who connects two developmental factors:

> *Physical and communication skills develop from birth in the context of interaction and engagement. One example of this is the development of visual skills, essential for literacy, numeracy and coordination ... There is more to vision than the sense of sight alone; coherent visual perception is the product of vision working together with other sensory systems entrained through the medium of movement. This is the physical process through which children learn to understand distance, depth and timing and develop the sequential eye movements needed for reading.*
>
> (Family and Childcare Trust, 2017, np)

It could be the case that parents are time-poor, so that opportunities for listening, reflecting, and responding patiently to their youngsters who may be struggling to express themselves, are increasingly constrained. It can be argued that work is urgently needed to raise awareness, provide understanding and develop the skills for action for parents and other carers to communicate with babies/toddlers in early infancy in particular. For example, there is growing concern that opportunities for engagement are lost if parents and carers increasingly connect with their smartphones, rather than with their infant children. In a recent survey commissioned by www.whataboutthechildren. org.uk, 79% agreed with the statement: "The use of mobile phones and social media distracts parents away from responding to their children" (What About the Children?, 2018).

But there are practical strategies which can facilitate and enhance parent/child communication. One suggestion comes out of Zeedyk's 2014 ground-breaking study of Carer-facing and Outward-facing buggies. In summary, when babies and toddlers face the adult pushing them, the extent and richness of communication between the two can be facilitated. In fact, Zeedyk's findings were so dramatic that a well-known manufacturer began to produce many more Carer-facing models. There could be other positive spin-offs of this, especially for babies. One is that the connective attachment process could be enhanced protection for the youngsters from the confusion and over-stimulation of traffic whizzing by (Zeedyk, 2014).

Early years settings: the critical importance of, and challenges for, the Key Person role in relation to secondary attachment

In the reality of a 21st century environment, for any consideration of pre-school children it is important now to look beyond home and family to examine provision in early years settings where the majority of these children spend a high proportion of their time. In relation to children's emotional well-being and its place as a pre-requisite for learning, it is important to ask: what is desirable? What do parents think is desirable? What are the challenges for early years practitioners? In short, are the holistic needs of the under 3s understood in theory and evident in practice?

A recent survey commissioned by What About the Children? (www.whataboutthechildren.org.uk, 2018) presented interesting results in relation to perceptions of early years education and care settings.

Thinking about children under 3 years old, how strongly do you agree or disagree with the following: Generally, the emotional development of the Under 3s is better achieved in a group setting like nurseries than at home with one to one care. When discounting the 'Don't Knows', net agreement with the statement was 59%. These Findings demonstrate high public confidence in staff in nursery settings being able to provide care for the Under 3s, accounting for their emotional needs.

For some time, the benefits of the Key Person role have been recognised as critical to children's well-being in early years settings and this is exemplified in the Early Years Foundation Stage guidance (EYFS) (Department for Education, 2017). Bearing in mind the above discussion regarding the critical importance of one to one emotional engagement, first and foremost this role must be about the relationship between each young child and the designated person who will provide reassurance and a sense of safety in an unfamiliar environment of non-parental care. Ideally, this practitioner/child relationship will be reliably sustained throughout the child's time in early years settings, especially for children under 3 years. Arguably this can be better sustained in family group arrangements rather than changes in the Key Person which may happen when children are in separate age and stage rooms. Whatever the arrangement, relationships of trust between the key persons and the parents should be established early on and sustained, initially through home visits, then through regular communication, via online platforms as well as face to face. Bronfenbrenner's emphasis on communication between systems and settings for all parties involved in infant care and education is explored elsewhere in this volume.

Primarily, the Key Person needs to be sensitive to the needs, feelings, and personality of each child allocated to them. However, the quality and reliability of provision will be highly dependent on several factors, including, for example, the culture of the early years setting, the skill and understanding of the practitioner, and on ratios. How many children are allocated to each practitioner and how much time they have for real engagement, so often affected by practical factors such as funding, sometimes makes impossible what would be ideal.

The term Key Carer is often preferred to Key Person (KP) as it places stronger emphasis on the nurturing element of the role. An awareness of separation anxiety experienced by young children and the importance of establishing relationship security will cement the KP role in the attachment process, promoting a sense of belonging for the child outside the parental home. It is important also that practitioners are alert to the impact of stress on the infant brain. In this regard, Goldschmied and Jackson (2003, p 42) urge early years staff to remember that

> *a child, and particularly a young and almost totally dependent ... is the only person in the nursery who cannot understand why he is there. He can only explain it as abandonment, and unless he is helped in a positive and affectionate way, this will mean levels of anxiety greater than he can tolerate.*

But with sound connection with a significant adult, who understands the foundational need for continued bonds of attachment, the child will be a secure child, open to new experiences and motivated to connect, to communicate, and to learn. We underestimate the importance of emotional security in early provision for children under three only at great cost to their futures. The third birthday is something of a milestone, for, by then, 80% of the brain's development will have happened. It is therefore critically important for both parents and practitioners to understand how "the early brain is shaped in the intimacy of care" (Ulanowsky and Pereira-Gray, 2015, p 6).

Some snapshots from students on placement in early years settings indicate the variability of views around provision to support best practice:

Student 1
"The Key Person will ensure that the care of the child is tailored to their individual needs. This builds positive relationships as the child will form a bond with this practitioner who will know how to accelerate their development."

Student 2
"I was allocated a child of 22 months while on Placement. There were several incidents when the child seem to desire human contact which was only sometimes available, and sometimes not."

Student 3

"When Child B, aged 14 months, entered the nursery they were uneasy in their new surroundings. They would not play or explore and would only be calm when sat on the practitioner's knee – or they would become hysterical."

In the early part of life, right brain development, which has critical bearing on children's social and emotional development, predominates. The right brain also serves to regulate stress (or otherwise). Emotional stress generates steroid production which can harm the developing brain (Pereira Gray, 2013; Schore, 2014). Evidence is clear that sustained stress in infancy generates an over-production of the hormone cortisol when sensitive nervous systems are being formed, having a significantly negative impact.

Cortisol, sometimes termed the flight, fight, or freeze hormone, is generated by the brain at times of stress. Experiences of short-duration stress triggering bursts of this hormone are not of concern, even for very young infants whose brain development is highly sensitive to neurochemicals in the body. However, problems occur when stress is chronic and persistent, causing de-regulation of brain and body systems, with likely implications for early learning and for an individual's mental health and well-being into the future (Sigman, 2011).

The level and fluctuation of cortisol levels in the infant brain can now be captured simply and non-invasively, even from very young children, from saliva swabs taken at different times of the day. For both adults and children, the natural pattern is for cortisol levels to be highest in the morning, diminishing during the day, with lowest levels in the evening. We have long been aware that children cared for in chaotic households and/or with violent or unresponsive carers are subject to high levels of stress causing negative spin-offs for present and future emotional and mental health. However, no such dangers have been anticipated for the safety and organisational reliability of paid for care in professional settings. Until now. Some concerning behavioural signs for very young children spending substantial parts of their days in group care has triggered important studies utilising the saliva swab method to measure levels and fluctuations in cortisol production.

In the United States, Watamura et al.'s (2010) ground-breaking research into the impact of childcare on cortisol secretion was with children attending three different daycare centres, each rated as "good to excellent". Samples of saliva taken throughout each day were compared with samples taken at the weekend when the children were at home. The samples were tested for cortisol levels and also for an antibody called immunoglobulin A, part of the body's immune system to fight infectious agents which can be undermined by episodes of acute stress. Of concern is that persistently-raised cortisol levels were detected in tests taken in the afternoon period in daycare, contrasting with normally expected patterns.

Of further concern was the decrease in antibody secretion correlating with these raised cortisol levels.

A further, more recent study sought to measure comparative cortisol levels when young infants were in daycare and, alternatively, at home by family members. This study took place in 85 different childcare centres in Norway by Drugli et al. (2017). The toddlers were split into two groups, the first having 5–7 hours in non-parental care, the second 8–9 hours. For both groups, when in non-parental care, gradually increasing cortisol levels throughout the day were found. However, it was the children in the second group who had spent the longest time in day care who registered the highest readings overall.

In summary, children under 3 years cared for in chaotic households and/or by parents unresponsive to their needs, or in poor quality settings, offering very limited one to one interaction and/or interrupted carer/child relationships making secondary attachments difficult to establish, are at risk. Also at risk from raised cortisol levels, are babies and toddlers spending long hours in daycare, even when these children are apparently calm and settled. Practitioner understanding of the impact of stress on the infant brain (through an over-production and persistently high level of cortisol) should be part of early years education and training.

Psychologist Zeedyke (n.d.) asserts that all practitioners need to have "a very good understanding of the science of *connection*" (my italics). Importantly she reminds us that children are "biologically programmed to be scared of strangers". For this reason, every child needs to have *familiarity with and confidence in*, a special carer who takes over from family away from the intimacy of home. Transitions from home to setting at the beginning and end of the day can be especially "anxiety provoking" for a young child which, if oft repeated without resolution, can get "permanently wired into the brain". Zeedyke (n.d.) asserts that everything that happens, or does not happen, for a young child can leave a psychological trace in the growing brain.

Peter Elfer, Principal Lecturer in early years at the University of Roehampton is of the view that the role of Key Persons is one required to monitor and measure, at the same time to build emotional bonds with the children in their care (Elfer, 2018). But, he asserts, practitioners must maintain an emotional distance. For all that, when Dr Jules Page (What About The Children, 2018) poses an important question to early years professionals: "Should Early Years professionals love the children in their care, and how can they show that love?" the majority of professionals agreed, being of the view that showing affection for children, including through touch, is an important part of professional practice. However, some expressed worries: "It can be considered not the 'done thing' to show affection to children, even though we know they need it". This PLEYS project (Professional Love in Early Years Settings) was conducted at the Centre for Research in Early Childhood Education at the University of Sheffield, in collaboration with a London-based group of nurseries with practices underpinned by Bowlby's Attachment theory. Following this study, an "Attachment Toolkit" has been developed and is available online (www.whataboutthechildren.org.uk /downloads/conference/2016).

Touch is a powerful non-verbal message that someone is connecting with you and caring about you. With safeguarding systems in place in care and education settings, physical touch – being held by a familiar carer – is an essential requirement for a young child, not least when upset or anxious. In general terms, there is considerable research to suggest that the younger the child, the more important is the provision of consistent, informed, responsive and committed one-to-one input, whatever the setting. However, this may not always happen.

> Student 4 (Note in her Placement Diary)
> "Today, during snack time, Child A looked very tired and unhappy. I approached him and asked if he was alright. Child A nodded but reached up and put his hands around my neck and asked me to pick him up. He then said, 'Can you sit next to me?' I picked him up and we went over to the snack table. Once I had sat down he wanted to sit on my knee. One of the key workers heard Child A and said 'You need to sit on your chair please'. I then placed Child A on his own chair but I moved my own chair closer to him as I believe that made him feel that I cared for and valued him."

In Chapter 6 Gripton emphasises the importance of responding to each child's individual characteristics, needs and perspectives. In a sense being "held in mind" by a significant adult in important ways mimics the critical parental role, but this is a secondary attachment, which in no way should undermine the primary attachment between parent and child. Yet, even with safeguards in place, some parents feel uneasy about another individual getting too close to their child and therefore will seek group care in a nursery, even for their babies of less than a year old, rather than a childminder, for precisely this reason (What About the Children, 2012)

Childcare external to the family is increasingly measured and controlled. Arguably, over the past decade or so, whilst quality may be better assured, there is evidence to suggest that the early years environment remains significantly influenced by the twin pressures of the "education zeitgeist" and the "economic nexus". It can be argued therefore that the developmental needs of the under 3s who need significant amounts of one to one communication with, and continuity of care by, familiar practitioners, are denied, as staffing levels become ever more constrained by inadequate funding, and practice is ever more driven by the school readiness requirement for older age-groups. There is strong research evidence for a different model of provision for the under 3s, sensitive to their attachment needs, a view strongly endorsed by the World Association for Infant Mental Health (2014).

One could argue that ensuring and sustaining optimum development for every child through adequate ratios of staff to children is a social justice issue. Failure to deliver optimum child development becomes a fundamental failure to address human rights. Ensuring conditions for healthy emotional development is critical and early disadvantage causes a delay in language acquisition, impacting on learning and development, reverberating into a child's future. In summary, the quality of earliest relationships will have critical impact on whether children will flourish, or otherwise.

Values and practices through time – Bronfenbrenner's ecological system

After parents and grandparents, arguably, the most important influences in a child's life will be early years practitioners assisting children's critical progression from Bronfenbrenner's micro to meso system. Appropriate recognition of the true worth of adults central in a child's early life is critical. Yet these most important people often remain of low status and are poorly remunerated.

Specific values underpin the mores of everyday life influencing how we prioritise and interpret our various roles. We might ask how the interpretation of Bronfenbrenner's 1979 ecological systems – the interconnectedness between a child and her environment – might compare with that of a 2018 context: what assumptions about children are made in each case? It is interesting to note how, in more recent literature on early years practice, that childcare external to the family is now incorporated into Bronfenbrenner's micro-system, formerly designated to family only (Gray and Mac Blain, 2015). The truth is that children's needs remain pretty much the same through time and context. Adequate nutrition and protection in a responsive and stimulating environment; being cared for by adults who have knowledge about, and sensitivity to, their emotional and developmental needs, are critical factors. Most of all, children's needs should be prioritised by the most important people in their lives and prioritised too by government, who, in several ways, through the macro-system of policy, sets the context of childhood experience. Three decades ago, we were instructed by the UN Convention on the Rights of the Child (UNCRC) (1989) that children should have a voice on matters which concern them. We need to ask what these voices might say.

It is the case that each of what Bronfenbrenner terms "circles of influence" are influenced by culturally dominant/time-specific values and mores. Fiscal policy in any context needs to raise taxes to provide services and, at the end of the day, to balance the economic books. Alongside, ideologically influenced approaches to provision will impact significantly on education and social policy. One can wonder if the carrot of free or subsidised childcare to encourage mothers back into the workplace sooner than they might choose is not entirely Treasury-led?

In turn, one can wonder if explicit tax and benefit rewards of taking up paid work, and a valorising of Working Mums over Non-working Mums (a misnomer if ever there was one) into "deserving" and "non-deserving" categories, has not overly influenced public consciousness and decision-making in ways disadvantageous to our youngest children. Mothers committed to nurturing their infant children in the first 30 months or so are frequently perceived as engaged in anti-feminist drudgery. Balancing the needs of mothers and their infants should be a matter of what is best for those most concerned regarding the how, the what, and the when of care. However, it is recognised that many parents do not have the economic choice to do what they think is best for their children and themselves. There is not space here to explore these matters further (but see Ulanowsky, 2008). It is just as important to say emphatically that feminism and mothering need not be mutually exclusive categories.

There are critical developmental periods for a young child's development. The infant brain doubles in size in the first year of life, it is highly malleable and moulded by early experience which literally shapes the brain's architecture impacting on intellectual competence and psycho/physical health, lifelong (Ulanowsky and Pereira-Gray, 2015). However, lack of awareness of the holistic requirements of early infancy, lack of resources to support parents in their nurturing task, and lack of systems to disseminate information and provide important training to professionals called upon to deliver care and education can mean that generations to come may be affected in ways we would not choose (Pereira Gray, 2013). Yet, in some ways, early years settings for the under 3s are inclined to reflect an increasing focus on competency targets being primarily directed towards cognitive development. Those committed to the development of the whole child bewail lack of time and opportunity to enjoy exploratory play and activities for building trust in themselves and relationships with others. However, an over-structuring of children's lives has been evident for some time. Two decades ago, research conducted by Jacqui Cousins, UN Advisor on Early Education, recorded children as complaining of being too hurried in their lives and compelled, by overly aspirational parents, always to engage in "structured" and "educational" activities rather than being allowed space for what they would wish to do: "All the time it's 'Hurry up, Hurry up!'... I hate hurrying up!" (Cousins, 1999, p 35). This theme is echoed in discussion in later chapters, especially Chapter 6.

Over a century ago Charles Darwin discovered it is not the strongest of the species that survives, nor the most intelligent, but the one most responsive to change. In turn, Bowlby found it is the most securely attached infants who are the ones displaying confident adaptability to new situations. In turn, educators find that effective learners have the inner confidence to reflect and act on what they know, and what they do not know. An extensive longitudinal study conducted by the London School of Economics found the majority of adults were of the view that their emotional health in childhood was the most important predictor of their life satisfaction in adulthood (Clark et al., 2014). For all that, we continue to prioritise education over care, and perhaps too, pre-schoolers over babies, failing to recognise that it is the quality of early input that makes all the difference.

The influence of the early communication environment within the microcosm of the family will lessen through time BUT early experiences will impact life-long. Care and education settings will then seek to sustain a vibrant communication environment responsive to each child's needs. Alertness to the developmental factors which can impede or enhance this will be critical.

PROVOCATIONS

■ How convinced are you of the close connection between emotion and cognition?

■ To what extent would Family Groupings in early years settings – promote secondary attachment by sustaining the connection between Key Persons and the children for whom they are responsible?

■ How does effective communication support the cohesion and care in early years settings?

■ Do you think the under 3s should be prioritised in terms of staffing and funding?

References

Abrams, D.A. et al., 2016. Neural circuits underlying mother's voice perception predict social communication abilities in children. *Proceedings of the National Academy of Sciences*, 113 (22), 6295–6300.

Barlow, J., 2018. Maternal representations in pregnancy: Importance of the mothers' relationship with their unborn babies. In: P. Leach, ed. *Transforming infant well-being - research, policy and practice for the first 1001 critical days*. Oxford: Routledge, pp. 37–46.

Baron-Cohen, S., 2012. *Zero degrees of empathy*. London: Penguin.

Beuchemin, M. et al., 2010. Mother and stranger: An electrophysiological study of voice processing in newborns. *Cerebral Cortex*, 21 (8), 1705–1711.

Bronfenbrenner, U., 1979. *The ecology of human development*. Harvard: Harvard University Press.

Chomsky, N., 1976. *Reflections on language*. London: Fontana.

Clark, A.E., Layard, R., Cornaglia, F., Powdthavee, N., and Vernoit, J., 2014. What predicts a successful life? A life-course model of well-being. *The Economic Journal*, 124 (580), F720.

Clegg, J. et al., 2015. The contribution of early language development to children's emotional and behavioural functioning at 6 years: an analysis of data from the Children in Focus sample from the ALSPAC birth cohort. *Journal of Child Psychology and Psychiatry*, 56 (1), 67–75.

Cousins, J., 1999. *Listening to four year olds: How they can help us plan their education and care.* London: The National Early Years Network.

Department for Education, 2017. *Early Years Foundation Stage Statutory Framework (EYFS).* Available at: https://www.gov.uk/government/publications/early-years-foundation-stage-framework--2 [Accessed 27.03.2018].

Dewar, G., 2018. *The social abilities of newborns: why babies are born to learn from our sensitive, loving care.* Available at: https://www.parentingscience.com/newborns-and-the-social-world.html [Accessed 17.05.2018].

Drugli, M.B., Solheim, E., Lydersen, S., Moe, V., Smith, L., and Berg-Nielsen, T.S., 2017. Elevated cortisol levels in Norwegian toddlers in childcare. *Early Child Development and Care*, 188 (12), 1684–1695.

Elfer, P., 2015. Love is no longer all you need. *Nursery World* [online]. Available at: https://www.nurseryworld.co.uk/nursery-world/opinion/1151537/love-is-no-longer-all-you-need [Accessed 31.03.2018].

Eliens, M., 2016. The importance of the first hour of bonding and the year after. Summary of paper given at conference, (March 10, 2016), London. *Cracking the code – young children are born ready to communicate, but they need a translator.* March 10, London. www.whataboutthechildren.org.uk [Accessed 01.04.2018].

Family and Childcare Trust, 2017. Available at: https://familyandchildcaretrust,org.uk [Accessed 15.08.2018].

Goldschmied, E., and Jackson, S., 2003. *People under 3.* Oxford: Routledge.

Gray, C., and Mac Blain, S.C., 2015. *Learning theories of childhood.* London: Sage.

Guinn, A.S., Lutzker, J.R., and Chaffin, M., 2018. Safecare, the case for parent-infant language training. In: P. Leach, ed. *Transforming infant well-being - research, policy and practice for the first 1001 critical days.* Oxford: Routledge, pp. 215–223.

Howe, D., 2011. *Attachment across the lifecourse: A brief introduction.* New York: Palgrave Mc Millan.

Kindsley, C.H., Tujuba, H., and Meyer, E.E.A., 2011. When mothers go wrong: Likely neural undercurrents related to poor parenting. *Frontiers in Psychiatry* [online], 2 (26). Available at: https://www.frontiersin.org/articles/10.3389/fpsyt.2011.00026/full [Accessed 04.06.2018].

Kuhl, P.K., 2011. Early Language and Literacy: Neuroscience implications for education. *Mind, Brain and Education*, 5 (3), 128–142.

Leach, P., 2018. Introduction: Fifty years of childhood. In: P. Leach, ed. *Transforming infant well-being - research, policy and practice for the first 1001 critical days.* Oxford: Routledge, pp 3–10.

Mileva-Seitz, V., Afonso, V.M., and Fleming, A.S., 2013. Dopamine: Another "Magic Bullet" for caregiver responsiveness?. In: D. Narvaez, J. Panksepp, A.N. Schore, and T. Gleason, eds. *Evolution, early experience and human development.* Oxford: Oxford University Press, pp. 152–178.

Murray, L., and Cooper, P., 2018. Post-natal depression and the under twos. In: P. Leach, ed. *Transforming infant well-being - research, policy and practice for the first 1001 critical days.* Oxford: Routledge, pp. 56–66.

Pawlby, S., 2018. Keeping the baby in mind: offspring of mothers with perinatal severe mental illness. *The never-changing emotional needs of the under threes conference.* March,London.[online].Availableat:http://www.whataboutthechildren.org.uk/images/documents/Offspring-of-mothers-with-pre-natal-mental-illness_Sue-Pawlby.pdf [Accessed 29.09. 2018].

Pereira Gray, D., 2013. *It's the relationships, stupid!* [online]. London: Third Goodman Lecture. Available at: http://www.whataboutthechildren.org.uk/downloads/conference-2013/goodman_lecture_2013.pdf [Accessed 29.09.2018].

Social Innovation Generation. Available at: www.sigeration.ca/?s=roots+of+empathy [Accessed 15.11.18].

Schore, A., 2014. *The science of the art of psychotherapy.* Masterclass given at Centre for Emotional Development, University of Brighton (23 September 2014).

Sigman, A. 2011. Mother superior? The biological effects of daycare. *The Biologist*, 58 (3), 29–32.

Ulanowsky, C., 2008. *Women as mothers: Changing role perceptions. An intergenerational study.* PhD Thesis, Open University.

Ulanowsky, C., and Pereira-Gray, D., 2015. *Infant mental health: Factors affecting optimal development.* London: Evidence for Enquiry. All Party Parliamentary Group on Children (The First 1001 Days). Available at: www.whataboutthechildren.org.uk [Accessed 20.06.18].

Unicef, 1989. *The United Nations Convention on the Rights of the Child.* London: Unicef. Available at: https://www.unicef.org.uk/what-we-do/un-convention-child-rights

Watamura, S.E., Coe, C.L., Laudenslager, M.L., and Robertson, S.S., 2010. Childcare setting affects salivary cortisol and antibody secretion in young children. *Psychoneuroendochrinology*, 35 (8), 1156–1166.

What About the Children?, 2012. Childcare provision for the under-threes. Poll of mums with children under 3. WATCH Media Report, November, 2012. Contact: www.whataboutthechildren.org.uk for full survey report. Tel: 0845 602 7145.

What About The Children?, 2016. Professional love in early years settings – a collaborative approach. *Cracking the code – young children are born ready to communicate but they need a translator.* March 10, London. Online summary available at: www.whataboutthechildren.or.uk/downloads/conference- 2016/2016-jools-page--john-warren-summary.pdf [Accessed 29.09.2018].

What About The Children?, 2018. Raising children in the 21st Century. www.whataboutthechildren.org.uk/advocacy [Accessed 1.11.18].

World Association of Infant Mental Health (WAIMH), 2014. *Position paper on the rights of infants*, University of Tampere, Finland.

Zeedyk S., (n.d.). Childcare practice. Available at: http://www.suzannezeedyk.com/childcare-practice-suzanne-zeedyk/ [Accessed 31.03.2018].

Zeedyk, S., 2014. *How buggies shape babies' brains.* Available at: http://suzannezeedyk.co.uk/wp2/2014/04/03 [Accessed 16.04.18].

Suggested websites

www.parentsasfirstteachers.org.uk
www.Readit2
www.rootsofempathy.org
www.SaveChildhoodMovement:
www.whataboutthechildren.org.uk

3 Communicating children's perspectives

Catherine Gripton

OVERVIEW OF CHAPTER

This chapter explores the ways in which children's perspectives can be represented, valued, and acted upon within early education. It considers education as experienced by the child rather than as intended by adults and suggests that children's perspectives are significantly underrepresented in education. In this chapter child voice is considered within the context of children's participatory rights and it is argued that children's perspectives offer practitioners a way to genuinely listen to children and to better understand their highly individual experiences. It develops the theme of attending to all children's perspectives and provides a range of approaches which can be used to help practitioners and setting leaders better understand children's perspectives and use this crucially important knowledge to evaluate and reflect upon practice and provision. The chapter concludes by indicating the importance of creating a culture within settings of active attention to children's perspectives, suggesting that this supports educational improvement and is beneficial to all involved – not least the children.

Introduction

Children's views are significantly underrepresented in educational research, in education, and in society. Children can be perceived as not ready or capable of contributing to what is typically an adult-centred debate, system, or approach. This is often deemed an issue of communication and competency. Children are not deemed proficient in the modes of communication used and valued by research, education, and society, and additionally not capable of forming a fully valid viewpoint; "as unreliable witnesses about their own lives" (Qvortrup et al. 1994, p. 2). This perception of children as deficient in adultness or 'adults in waiting' is incongruent with the view of children as capable and competent which most practitioners subscribe to. If we accept that children's and adults' worlds are different then it seems unfair to exclude or sideline children's views because they do not fit with adult ways of understanding, particularly as it is the children's education under consideration.

One of the issues leading to the lack of children's voices in education is the narrow range of communication modes utilised which often preclude children's perspectives. As I point out in Chapter 6 we tend to focus upon spoken and written word in education and research. Another key issue is the focus upon asking for a child's view or opinion rather than seeking to understand their standpoint or perspective. This requires a quite adult-like understanding of education and typically seeks a view or an answer for an adult priority or question. A third, fundamental issue is the lack of full representation within views sought. Typically, a consultative model is employed where a sample of views are included which produces a skew where some children and their families are listened to more than others. These three big issues are explored in this chapter and a range of possible approaches are presented which focus upon children's perspectives instead of children's views as this provides a way forwards which, it is argued, is potentially more inclusive, authentic, and effective.

Voices or perspectives?

Too often a focus upon child voice has been a focus upon children's opinions, a consultation on specific issues from the adult perspective, rather than seeking their perspectives, thus achieving a more holistic understanding of their lived experiences and genuine involvement in settings from the child's perspective. Seeking perspectives involves more of a participatory than a consultative approach. Perspectives require children to be cognisant and active participants within their setting with their perspectives integrated within the fabric of how the setting operates, whereas consultation or voice can involve children without their full awareness or merely include their presence and can lead to a patchy or piecemeal involvement in a typically adult-initiated activity (Hill 2006). Within consultation, children and families are often offered the opportunity to contribute but not all will have the time, confidence, or motivation to do so. We need, therefore, to be cautious that enthusiasm and a deep respect for children's participation in all aspects of their education does not become an intermittent or separate focus upon a narrow notion of a single and simplified "child voice" with the illusion of participation (Palaiologou 2014).

Older children's views are typically more likely to be sought than younger children's within a drive to make provision for child voice in education settings with a focus upon spoken and written communication of views. Gripton (2014, p. 82) provides a cautionary tale of the illusion of participation with older children. It describes a child who became disenfranchised with being a representative for her class in a primary school council when she realised that they had no real efficacy and their opinions could be easily dismissed by adults. Measures to promote child voice can be tokenistic because they are separate additions to provision which are not fully embedded within the setting or because they are limited in scope. Child voice is an illusion where the children do not believe they will be listened to or that their feelings or ideas can contribute to the potential for change. Similarly, child voice is an illusion where children communicate what they think the adults want to hear or feel that their views will be enacted selectively dependent upon alignment with adult views. A focus upon child voice, therefore, risks the appearance of child participation without it ever being realised.

If we are to genuinely listen to children and recognise them as social agents who are active participants in society, making choices about their lives, then we need to be ready to listen to what they say in all of their modes of communication and not just what we want to hear. This requires an alternative approach to seeking their views and requires a continually open forum that is grounded within the child's world. Children should not be expected to be adults and engage in adult modes of communication, reflect upon adult priorities, and make adult choices or decisions. The purpose of listening to children's perspectives is not to accelerate them towards adulthood. Listening to the hundred languages of children and childhood (Malaguzzi in Edwards, Gandini, and Forman 2012), we instead need an approach which enables continual attention to *children's perspectives*.

The importance of children's perspectives

Children's perspectives are integral in shaping their education and are important as they enact their rights and recognise them as competent social agents but also because they are the most knowledgeable people about education. As Harcourt (2011) points out, children are the experts in being children so their perspectives are invaluable to practitioners and education more generally. In order to really listen and take account of these perspectives, we need to consider each child's individual lived experiences. The focus upon lived experience is crucial as it recognises that perspectives are based upon what a child experiences rather than the provision offered within the environment or the practitioner perception of the provision. It is the individual internal meaning constructed from a child's everyday interactions with their environment and other people. This can be really challenging for us as practitioners as we shift our thinking from what we provided and intended, to what the child actually noticed and made sense of.

Case Study 1 describes a mathematics session observed in an early years setting with the perspectives of the practitioner and the child interpreted by an observer. It suggests an apparent disconnect between the practitioner perception of a child's educational experience and the child's lived experience of it. Essentially, it seems that they have perceived the same situation differently. Nathan has not really engaged in any mathematical thinking, despite the mathematical focus intended for the session and the resources. This example reminds us to question whether opportunities for learning and development actually exist if the child does not experience them. The implications for provision are that we need to provide multiple opportunities in a range of contexts to maximise the likelihood that an aspect of learning will be present within the possibilities experienced by the individual child. A "maths area", for example, cannot be the only opportunities for mathematical learning perceived by the practitioner as the child may not visit this area or may not engage in mathematics when they do (see Gripton 2017 for an example of this happening in a "maths area").

CASE STUDY I

Nathan's Guns

Miss Carr's perspective: Nathan came to sit on the carpet with the twelve other children when the tidy up music finished and I pointed him to a spot near to me to ensure that he listened. We all sang the days of the week song and Nathan nodded along and made the signs for the days of the week with his fingers. All of the children counted to thirteen together as I pointed to the names of the children here today and Nathan counted to thirteen accurately. I modelled how to count thirteen using plastic cubes and Nathan was really interested. He asked for the stick of thirteen cubes at the end of number time and continued to play with them during free play. He moved the cubes into several different arrangements and pointed to count that he had thirteen for each different arrangement he made.

Nathan's perspective: I followed my friend Caiden when he stopped playing in the water and walked away. I wanted to sit next to him before anyone else did but Miss Carr pointed to the floor next to her so I sat there. She had her cowboy boots on again. Through the window, I spotted some birds flying in the sky and remembered the "shoot 'em down" music from my computer at home. I sang it in my head and nodded my head in time to the song. I made a gun with my hand and pretended to shoot at each one. Miss Carr asked me a question and I nodded. She got some cubes to build with – I like building and watched her build a rifle with them. She showed me the rifle and said "furteen" and looked at me. I nodded to tell her that I wanted them and copied her, saying "furteen". Miss Carr smiled and I smiled – she is nice. When Caiden went to play, I asked Miss Carr if I could have the cubes and she let me. I made them into a gun with a handle and put pretend bullets in by pushing my finger on the cubes. I made a gun with two handles then a gun with two bits to shoot out of. I liked making the guns and putting the bullets in with my finger. I am going to take my gun with me at home time and show it to my brother.

Whilst clearly a less subtle example, it can be quite unnerving for us as we consider what children actually make meaning of and assimilate within their lived experience compared to what they were present for and perhaps what we intended. Listening to children in an early years setting is therefore much more than hearing what they say. It is fundamentally about careful attention to their perspective and must include considerable effort to gain an understanding of the individual experiences of each child: to know something of what it is like to be them in this place. This question is at the heart of the Mosaic approach (Clark 2005). Holistic, observation-led assessment and documentation are a key way in which practitioners achieve this in early years settings. We spend time watching, playing with, conversing with, and listening to children to assist us in understanding their world as they experience it. Listening to children, as attention to children's perspectives, is therefore active instead of passive, and is an ethos which underpins practice.

Lived experience is layered emotions, actions, and conceptions (Løndal 2010) and is internal so we can only ever partially understand the lived experience of another (Pálmadóttir and Einarsdóttir 2016). Each child's lived experience is shaped by their individual ecology, the unique interacting contextual layers around the child of Bronfenbrenner (1979). For Nathan, in Case Study 1, his lived experiences of home, family, and education contexts shaped his experience in the number session through the emotional, physical, and social connections that he made between these lived experiences and the opportunities in the environment at that moment. His previous lived experiences drew his attention and shaped his response to the birds he saw through the window, to Caiden as an important person to him and to the resources offered to him by the practitioner. Other children in the same session will each have attended differently to these stimuli and made different connections to their own lived experiences.

Children make many connections, a "whirlpool of associations" (Piaget 1977, p. 3), between a stimulus and their current thinking, formed as meaning they made from lived experiences. They assimilate (connect and integrate), accommodate (adapt and develop current thinking), or equilibrate (form new understanding) new experiences into existing schemes or internal structures which form their understanding of the world (Piaget 1977). Learning is associative and therefore connected to and building upon previous understandings which are highly individual. Assessment and curriculum materials often include typical or expected lines of progression but it is up to practitioners to recognise that each child has their own learning pathway. Within this, new learning is connected to the meaning made by each individual child of their lived experiences. Attention to children's perspectives is vitally important for practitioners in both scaffolding learning and listening to children.

Listening to all children's perspectives

In attending to their perspectives in order to listen to children, there is a tendency for some children's perspectives to be "heard" more than others. This is partly due to notions of representation within a consultation model discussed in the "voices or perspectives?" section of this chapter, where a few children's perspectives are deemed to represent all of the children. Even where every child's perspective is included, some children's tend to dominate practitioner thinking. If a child's parents are particularly communicative or if a child seeks out practitioners in the setting more regularly, there is a tendency to know more of their experiences.

Whilst we, instinctively know that children are each unique individuals with their own experiences, there is a tendency to group children's perspectives together and report these as, "children feel …", "children choose …", "the children like …", or "children need …". This is not exclusive to children, as both practitioner and parent views are commonly presented as a single voice. Even where we are more precise, in education we commonly make statements such as "the boys need …" or "the lower attainers can't …" attributing a unified perspective to all children deemed to have a specific adult-identified characteristic. It is a challenge to take account of all children's perspectives and can require practitioners, within a pedagogy of listening (Rinaldi 2006), to seek out opportunities and ways to understand each child's lived experience.

Children who use more spoken or written communication might be more readily apparent to practitioners as their perspectives might seem more accessible to us as adults. This quietens the perspectives of many children, particularly those identified as having additional or more complex needs whose perspectives can be defined by labels which can lead to often heard statements such as "children with autism …" or "children with Down's syndrome …". Knowledge of resources and strategies which have been successful for other children with the same "label" or "diagnosis" can be helpful to practitioners and parents. It is, however, important that these remain distinct from the child's individual perspective so that the child does not become defined by this label and their individual preferences, personality and experiences still valued. Sometimes, a child deemed to have additional needs might have their voice deferred to adults and be spoken *for* where well-meaning adults "interpret" and advocate for a child instead of seeking their individual perspective. Essentially, children's agency is reduced two-fold where their perspectives are deemed more difficult to communicate, particularly with signing or communication aids, and their choices reduced by the multiple and specific nature of their needs (Gripton and Hall 2016).

Children whom society deems most vulnerable are particularly at risk of their perspectives becoming lost amidst multiple adult voices, documentation, and processes. This perception of vulnerability is premised upon a lack of relative power, status, and currency within society and particularly affects children and their families with lower incomes and children not meeting education benchmarks or qualification thresholds. Cultural capital can act as leverage for those that have it where the perspectives of children and families with the most cultural capital have the greatest influence within education. As practitioners, we sometimes have to work harder to ensure that we listen to the individual perspectives of children and their families that are deemed most vulnerable.

Attention to children's perspectives can reveal significant differences in the sense they have made of the setting. Case Study 2 demonstrates two children's experiences of school and suggests that their lived experiences of classroom life are shaped by their attention to specific children whom they have strong relationships with. Their perspectives reveal an apparent yearning for wider collaborative opportunities from Freya and a comfort within the small group context from Christopher. Whilst both children's experiences are shaped by social aspects of the environment and important peer relationships, their perspectives are different. To change pedagogy within the classroom requires an understanding that Freya would relish the opportunity to collaborate and break out of the established groupings but Christopher might worry or withdraw somewhat, depending on whether his individual perspective is accounted for in the process of transition. Designing provision requires more than consulting children or considering the impact upon specific groups of children, but taking account of the individual perspectives of all children; a recognition of the plurality of children's perspectives.

CASE STUDY 2

Freya and Christopher's lived experiences of class groupings

Freya and Christopher appear to be keenly attentive to social aspects of classroom life. Peer relationships are very important to both and they frequently communicate with the researcher about their friends. Freya calls Abbie and Chloe, her "friend friends" suggesting that all children are referred to as "friends" in her class and therefore she seemingly distinguishes those in her inner circle using this term. Abbie and Chloe are in different groups to Freya and she naturally seems to notice what they are doing throughout the school day. She explains to the researcher which groups get different "work" to her and which adults work with each group. She makes inferences about the differences between the groups in terms of cleverness. She expresses some dissatisfaction at being in the group she is, explaining that she is "like too lonely on myself". Christopher's closest friends, Hal and Charlie, are in the same group as him and when asked what helps children to learn at school, he answered "our friends". Like Freya, Christopher is attentive to what his friends Hal and Charlie do throughout the day and communicates details about their endeavours. When communicating with the researcher, he does not mention adults in the classroom and when prompted explains that all children in the class get the same work (even though evidence suggests that the teacher gives out different tasks to different groups). Hal and Charlie feature significantly within Christopher's lived experience of his classroom. It seems that it is not the teacher's choices that impacted upon the children, more how they experienced these. For Freya, her attention was drawn to the other groups and therefore the differences she noticed there whereas for Christopher, his attention centred on his own group and the rest of the class featuring much less strongly within his lived experiences.

Communication is ultimately related to agency. Children can be denied agency where adults struggle to listen to, attend to or make sense of the child's perspective. A common approach to seeking children's perspectives can be through representation of a child's position or standpoint by an adult advocate; typically, a parent or practitioner. This indirect communication requires significant advocative abilities from adults if they are to consciously separate the child's perspective from their own, view from a child's world rather than an adult's world, and perhaps even advocate a viewpoint or priority that they do not necessarily agree with themselves. This is perhaps too much to ask of an adult with results being mediated or "second hand" at best. As practitioners, we need ways of gaining insight into and understanding of children's perspectives which requires not only attention to the full range of modes of communication that children use but also for us to provide opportunities for children to communicate their perspectives.

Approaches to illuminating children's perspectives

The notion of there being specific methods or practices which help us to elicit children's perspectives is a misnomer. There are many approaches that practitioners can use to help them gain insight into children's perspectives but ultimately it is the ethos of valuing children's perspectives rather than the activity itself that determines efficacy. As such, no one method or set of methods illuminate children's perspectives and any method can be utilised effectively if enacted with this principle at its heart (what Palaiologou 2014 terms "ethical praxis"). Participatory ways of working, where children are active participants in change processes, include children's perspectives by involving them in creating and evaluating aspects of their education. The examples included here can be used to gain additional insight into children's perspectives. They can be used within everyday practice as part of the fabric of the setting on an ongoing basis or alternatively can be used within a greater endeavour to shift power within a setting so that children are more actively engaged within the running and development of the setting and indeed have greater ownership of it. To be impactful, it is important that these are not isolated or short-term within a finite project but form part of a trajectory of listening to, attending to, and valuing children's perspectives. The following are examples offered within this understanding that illuminating children's perspectives is an enacted value and not a check list of specific set of activities. They draw upon practice where practitioners and researchers act upon a philosophical belief in the value, indeed necessity, of children's perspectives in education.

Guided tours

The physical environment can act as a mediator between adult and child (as I discuss in Chapter 6) and therefore be utilised effectively as a conduit to communicate children's perspectives. Using the familiar environment as a shared scaffold, children can give adults, other children, or a video camera a tour of the physical environment. Within a tour, what children point out or deem important can provide much insight. Their movement around the space and of use of resources communicates much in a way that can transcend the limitations of language and confidence. Where this is a paired or group endeavour, the negotiation, whether spoken or physical, between children over what to show, and what is important can be particularly illuminating. The familiarity and ownership connected to the environment as a shared space supports and sustains engagement. Within tours of "Children's lived places" (Raittila 2012) children share much more than the physical environment and resources; they share their lived experiences of this place. Tours can reveal much in terms of differences between perspectives as the environment, as the scaffold, is common for all involved but the children attend and connect to different aspects in different ways. Tours have been utilised effectively within research, for example in providing data for the research project in Case Study 2 and using tours of the locality of a setting in Raittila's study of children's lived experiences of their local environment.

Conversations

Conversations without an adult agenda, with a general focus (such as "why do you come to nursery?") or with an open-ended prompt (for example an image or a persona doll) can go in all manner of unanticipated directions. Interviews/conversations use a broader range of communication modes than merely the spoken. Non-verbal communication can sometimes communicate more than the verbal. Video is used by many practitioners to capture not only what is said by a child but *how* it is said although issues around consent and surveillance need careful attention (as discussed further by Cazaly in her chapter). Conversations with children can incorporate a wide range of prompts and resources which reveal much of the children's perspectives as they can enhance the power of the non-verbal communication. Having simple, open-ended resources or paper/whiteboard to hand when engaging in conversations allow the child to represent, draw, or map to help the practitioner to see what it is that the child wants them to know. Engaging in sustained shared conversations (Brown 2014) with children involves the co-construction of understanding and can highlight children's perspectives in a way that practitioners really understand as co-constructors themselves. Keeping records of conversations can aid practitioners in drawing together multiple pieces of evidence and building up evidence of children's perspectives. Often, these are documented as video or written notes. In a small-scale research project, children were asked which children they liked to play with and answers were recorded in a sociogram (a visual map of individuals' names/initials and lines/arrows to show connections). This record provided the practitioners with insight into the children's relationships as well as which children were chosen less frequently or not at all by other children, thus providing a valuable insight to act upon in practice.

Creations and representations

Creations and representations not only evoke creativity but enable an external representation of internalised experiences and therefore provide insight for practitioners into children's perspectives. Using imagination, they can also communicate perspectives as a child's ideas, desires, or wishes for idealistic or improved versions of the present. Whilst the resulting creation can reveal much, it is the process of creating that provides greater insight. The verbal and non-verbal communication, including pauses, adaptations, and facial expressions, alongside the creation process, highlights the child's lived experiences as they are drawn together into something new. Children can be encouraged to create in a huge range of ways that illuminate their perspectives including taking photographs, constructing, collaging (for example mood boards or wish lists), sorting/ ordering (photographs, images, or words), making sculptures, drawing, making maps, and painting. A simple request to draw or construct an early years setting, using the name the child uses for the setting, e.g. pre-school, nursery, can be illuminating. Drawings have been used effectively in research studies, for example MacDonald's study on children's experiences of starting school (2009), and have provided a content-rich way of children communicating their understanding, feelings, and experiences. The example in Case Study 2 arises from a research study where children were asked to make a representation of a classroom using small world toys. Freya's classroom representation showed children sitting in twos whereas Christopher's included a small group of children sitting closely together and other children dotted around. On their own, they provided some insight but when combined with the children's explanations of their representations as they made them, and also tours and interview conversations, they provided significant insight into the children's perspectives.

Observations

Observations are intrinsic to early years practice. More than an assessment record or tool, they are integral to pedagogy and an essential way in which practitioners know children. They clearly offer significant scope for illuminating children's perspectives and there are a range of observation methods and records which can be employed in doing so. Using a range of purposefully selected methods provides different structures for insight and therefore a fuller picture of children's perspectives. Whilst narrative observations are perhaps most common, timed observations, involving observations at regular intervals throughout a session, offer practitioners the opportunity to consider frequency of experience and balance between experiences for a child within a session. Tracking observations, where a map of the setting, indoor and outdoor, is annotated with the child's movement and sometimes timings and interactions, show which physical spaces a child visits most frequently. These can reveal the spaces and characteristics of spaces where a child feels most safe or comfortable, as well as the learning opportunities available to that the child given the spaces visited, in contrast to those offered across the whole setting.

Stories

Stories afford the opportunity to make connections, sequence ideas, and imagine when communicating children's perspectives. Stories can enable the child to communicate connections within their experiences so that practitioners gain insight into how the child feels or perceives the transitions in their day or the range of experiences engaged with. Whereas a tracking observation, for example, can show where a child visits within the physical environment, a story can communicate where a child would like to visit or would visit if it were adapted. Practitioners who work predominantly with one child have a greater sense than most of following one child's experience throughout their typical day in the setting. The story of one child's session can be documented by a practitioner and it can be enlightening to do so and fascinating as a setting leader for monitoring and evaluation purposes.

Through telling, acting, and representing stories, children can communicate how they would like things to be, or not to be, and they can exaggerate characters and feelings for dramatic effect in a way that adults get a clear sense of their understanding or feelings. Learning stories (Carr 2001) provide practitioners with a way of documenting children's learning in a positive child-friendly way so that it is shared and celebrated with other practitioners, children, and their families. It documents a sequence of learning as a story and there are many formats it might take often incorporating photographic and/or written interpretive evidence.

The communication of children's perspectives in educational settings

To listen to children means to attend to their perspectives and to value them. We need to adopt a pedagogy of listening to these perspectives which is woven into the fabric of our settings as well as our individual and shared values. This ethical praxis (Palaiologou 2014) is attentive to and respectful of all of the voices of the child (Malaguzzi's hundred languages of children; Malaguzzi in Edwards, Gandini, and Forman 2012) and all children's perspectives. This attention to children's perspectives is active rather than passive. It requires us, as practitioners, to utilise ways to illuminate children's perspectives (a few examples have been discussed in this chapter) and enact a persistent commitment to seeking all children's perspectives, particularly younger children, those with lower cultural capital and children identified as having additional needs.

Providing opportunities and creating a setting culture which is attentive to children's perspectives and actively seeks ways for these to be communicated to adults requires commitment from setting leaders as well as practitioners. Within the myriad of pressures upon settings, external and internal, to provide the very best education and care for young children, leaders can leap with haste to make changes to provision. This is only natural when wanting to do the very best for children and families but swift decisions can side-line perspectives, particularly those of children, within the decision-making process and poorer decisions can be made this way. Through attention to all children's perspectives and the many ways in which they are communicated, we can enable children to have far greater participation and agency within their education which will enhance the educational experience for practitioners, families, and, crucially, the children – the experts in early childhood education.

> **PROVOCATIONS**
>
> ◼ Why are children's voices or perspectives important in education and in society?
>
> ◼ What methods are most frequently used to communicate children's perspectives and what enables them to be effective in this? What methods could be utilised more and how could these be used most effectively?
>
> ◼ How can a focus upon children's perspectives be sustained and integrated into everyday practice?
>
> ◼ Which children's perspectives do we find most challenging to gain insight into and why is that?
>
> ◼ What are the beliefs and behaviours of an advocate for children's perspectives? What are the barriers to enacting these in practice and how can they be ameliorated?

References

Bronfenbrenner, U., 1979. *The Ecology of Human Development: Experiments by Design and Nature.* Cambridge, MA: Harvard University Press.

Brown, V., 2014. Sustained Shared Conversations. In: A. Woods, ed. *The Characteristics of Effective Learning: Creating and Capturing the Possibilities in the Early Years*, Oxon: Routledge, 2015, pp. 103–121.

Carr, M., 2001. *Assessment in Early Childhood Settings: Learning Stories.* London: Paul Chapman.

Clark, A., 2005. Ways of Seeing: Using the Mosaic Approach to Listen to Young Children's Perspectives. In: A. Clark, A.T. Kjorholt and P. Moss, eds., *Beyond Listening: Children's Perspectives on Early Childhood Services*. Bristol: Policy Press, 2005, pp. 29–50.

Edwards, C.P., Gandini, L., and Forman, G.E., eds., 2012. *The Hundred Languages of Children: The Reggio Emilia Experience in Transformation*. 3rd ed. Oxford: Praeger.

Gripton, C., 2014. Playing with Thinking. In: A. Woods, ed. *The Characteristics of Effective Learning: Creating and Capturing the Possibilities in the Early Years*, Oxon: Routledge, 2015, pp. 71–86.

Gripton, C., 2017. Planning for Endless Possibilities. In: A. Woods, ed., Child-initiated Play and Learning: Planning for Possibilities in the Early Years. 2nd ed. London: David Fulton, 2017, pp. 8–22.

Gripton, C. and Hall, V., 2016. Diverse Consumers. In: C. Hawkins, ed., *Rethinking Children as Consumers: The Changing Status of Childhood and Young Adulthood*. London: Taylor & Francis, 2016, pp. 11–29.

Harcourt, D., 2011. An Encounter with Children: Seeking Meaning and Understanding About Childhood. *European Early Childhood Education Research Journal*, 19 (1), 331–343.

Hill, M., 2006. Children's Voices on Ways of Having a Voice: Children's and Young People's Perspectives on Methods Used in Research and Consultation. *Childhood*, 13 (1), 69–89.

Løndal, K., 2010. Children's Lived Experience and Their Sense of Coherence: Bodily Play in a Norwegian After-school Programme. *Child Care in Practice*, 16 (4), 391–407.

MacDonald, A., 2009. Drawing Stories: The Power of Children's Drawings to Communicate the Lived Experience of Starting School. *Australasian Journal of Early Childhood*, 34 (3), 40–49.

Palaiologou, I., 2014. "Do We Hear What Children Want to Say?" Ethical Praxis When Choosing Research Tools with Children under Five. *Early Child Development and Care*, 184 (5), 689–705.

Pálmadóttir, H. and Einarsdóttir, J., 2016. Video Observations of Children's Perspectives on Their Lived Experiences: Challenges in the Relations Between the Researcher and Children. *European Early Childhood Education Research Journal*, 24 (5), 721–733.

Piaget, J., 1977. Problems of Equilibration. In: M.H. Appel, and L.S. Goldberg, eds., *Topics in Cognitive Development: Equilibration: Theory, Research, and Application*. Boston US: Springer, 1977, pp. 3–13.

Qvortrup, J., Bardy, M., Sgritta, G., and Wintersberger, H., 1994. *Childhood Matters: Social Theory, Practice and Politics*. Aldershot: Avebury.

Raittila, R., 2012. With Children in Their Lived Place: Children's Action as Research Data. *International Journal of Early Years Education*, 20 (3), 270–279.

Rinaldi, C., 2006. *In Dialogue with Reggio Emilia: Listening, Researching, and Learning*. London: Routledge.

Communication and learning dispositions

A formula for success

Sue Hobson and Caroline Farley

OVERVIEW OF CHAPTER

This chapter explores an innovative Communication Project carried out in a large university-based nursery offering care and early education to university staff and students' children aged from three months to five years old. The nursery is also open to children from the local town community. The nursery catchment is diverse both culturally and socially with many children learning English as an additional language. The project was delivered over 50 hours during a four-month period in late 2015.

Within this chapter the metaphor of chemical reaction is used, seeing the nursery environment as the crucible which hold the whole nursery community together, the people and buildings its separate chemical elements, and the trainer and project itself as the catalyst for the alchemy of permanent change. The chapter will consider the aspects of leadership and pedagogical approaches which supported the development of a learning community and which facilitated an enabling communication environment for both children and staff within this context.

The context: beyond the crucible

It is widely agreed in education practice and policy contexts that speech, language, and communication are crucial to every child's ability to access and get the most out of education and life. It is the chemistry, elements, and chain reaction that refines learning and development. It is the essential foundation for children's life, learning, and success (Dept for Education 2017). Consequently, Communication and Language have been the focus of reports, discussions, targeted interventions and concern for the government for many years.

Dame Tickell in her review of the Early Years Foundation Stage (EYFS) (2011) emphasises that it is essential that the early years workforce has the necessary skills to support and develop communication as "within the first years of the child's life, children have laid the ground work to becoming proficient in language which is the core of communication" (p 94). Indeed, there is nothing more important in early years education than the quality of the practitioners who are delivering it (DoE 2013). To that end, successive government's early years policy has focused on improving the qualifications, skills, and practice in all areas within the industry, with a variety of government training specifically focused on communication initiatives in particular.

Every Child a Talker (ECAT) (DCSF 2008), the national programme designed to raise young children's achievement in early communication and language and to improve practitioners' knowledge and skills, provided high-quality training and a level of ongoing accountability. However, training was largely accessed away from the nursery and followed a prescribed cascade model of delivery and implementation, and, whilst there have been successes, it has been less easy to track embedded change over time in communication culture across entire settings. The onus for ensuring continuing improvement in staff skills and practice is placed firmly on the manager's shoulders with the expectation that they provide effective and rigorous staff performance management and facilitate access to appropriate professional development (Ofsted 2015). Managers are held accountable for the achievement of excellence and are expected to manage this in the continuing culture and tradition of low status and low pay throughout the early years sector. Inherent within this challenge is a paradox for each and every manager. How to ensure individual and targeted staff development across a setting which, taken together, creates a community where the expectation of excellent practice is embedded and embraced by all?

Outline of the project

The Communication Project in this case was designed to address this need for a new approach by developing an enduring knowledge and understanding of communication and language in all practitioners that would be engraved on every aspect of daily practice. The project was shaped around the ELEYS study of effective pedagogy in the early years (Siraj-Blatchford and Manni 2007). Central to the project was the pedagogical belief that to improve practice required the co-construction and identification of shared objectives by practitioners across the setting team and the ability to inspire others with a vision of a better future. It required a level of dedication as well as the ability to reflect upon and engage with the changing context and utilise the passion about early years education that already existed. However, for this change to take place, a catalyst, a process in which atoms of the same or different elements rearrange themselves to form a new substance, was needed to initiate a reaction with the team.

The project was designed by the trainer to be delivered flexibly over 50 hours during a four month period. This allowed time, where necessary, for new skills to be practised and activities undertaken and the trainer to follow up and support the consolidation of learning. In contrast to traditional training programmes which tend to deliver training at a set time and in the same way to all staff, the timing and method of delivering learning opportunities in this project varied to accommodate all learners and was not pre-ordained but instead was responsive to perceived or changing need (see Figure 4.1). As McDonald et al. (2015) confirm in their research, a key to successfully embedding new learning from any form of training is the need for practitioners to have follow-up training and support to ensure any gains are sustained.

This flexible and reciprocal approach which was an integral part of the project design, relied on building strong relationships between trainer, managers, and practitioners, where practitioners were expected and encouraged to reflect and comment on their own learning and practice and identify the support, either group or individual, in specific areas that they felt they needed.

Another key element was that the project needed to be comparable to the cost of top down or "cascade" training for the whole team. It was designed to maximise sustainability and long-term cost effectiveness. The manager was aware of the risk of investing in an untested training package, but without a new way of working, evidence from past experience suggested that communication training would need to be revisited over and over again to re-educate each new member of staff individually rather than creating genuine and sustainable changes to the environment through embedded good practice. Here, the manager drew on Jago and Radford's (2016) research that suggests that collaborative practice creates better outcomes for children at an equal or lower cost than individuals working independently.

The Communication Project was designed to address evidence within the setting of inconsistencies in a practitioner's practice in the area of communication and language. Coburn (2003, p 6) states that "externally understood policies needs to become internally driven practice" and the impetus for the project recognised the mismatch between what practitioners suggested they knew and understood and what they actually implemented in relation to their communication practice. It aimed to develop a consistently skilled and reflective staff team across the nursery in this crucial area.

There was a firm belief rooted in the training approach that the proven effectiveness for young children of the principles and processes set out in the Early Years Foundation Stage (EYFS) (Department for Education 2017) and in the

Communication Project
Project description This project will enable all staff to develop their knowledge and understanding of the importance of communication and language in a young child's development. Staff will be confident using a wide range of strategies to support this in their daily practice with the children in their care. Learning throughout the project will be delivered using a range of teaching techniques in order to accommodate different learning styles.
Expected outcomes All staff will: • recognise good practice with regard to language and communication and be able to say why it is good • understand how to develop children's language for thinking • understand how to plan for and assess the development of children's language and communication and recognise when children have language difficulties • know that learning English as an additional language differs from learning a single language and be able to support children with EAL appropriately • be proficient in understanding and using visual systems to support children's understanding • be able to create an environment both inside and out that supports communication and language development • have created a bank of objects and visual prompts which are used consistently with the children throughout the session • have created a bank of objects and visual prompts to support group singing and story times • be confident in participating in Positive Peer Observations. A Communication Lead person will be identified for each age group who will work closely with the Project Leader and Nursery management and lead the delivery of excellent communication practice across the nursery
Activities • Whole group practical activities • Specific practice and activities with the children • Direct training on specific topics • Group and individual coaching • Room communication lead person training • Peer and leader observation and feedback
Individual activities During the project all staff will be expected to; • practise skills they have learned • take part in Positive Peer Observations in order to support colleagues as they practise new skills • fill in a Personal Learning Log and be prepared to share this with colleagues and project leaders.
Project evaluation Much of the evaluation of the project will be ongoing throughout in order to tailor the teaching to the needs of the staff and setting. Final evaluation will take place in the Autumn term against baseline information gathered prior to the start of the project. The project will be written up and shared with staff at the setting and with relevant managers at the University. Staff will have contributed to a Setting Communication Policy. A further visit will be undertaken to see how embedded in daily practice the learning has become and to address any areas that require further support.

Figure 4.1 The Communication Project rationale

guidance of Development Matters demonstrated a way that we all learn. Each and every staff member was viewed by the trainer and manager as a unique practitioner, having individual expertise and experience and this shaped the training package. For example, from the knowledge of how previous training had not been successfully embedded, it was recognised that the staff team would respond best to an active learning approach so a holistic approach to training was developed which required the engagement of all the senses to reinforce new ideas and concepts; this was the enabling environment.

Following early years principles, developing positive relationships, not only between colleagues but with the trainer, would optimise the learning. Parachute mentoring from the trainer would not be sufficient as Jopling et al. (2013, p 78) evidenced that mentoring such as provided in the ECAT programme is "not always sufficient to provide the 'extensive, sustained support which is characteristic of effective mentoring'".

An examination of the ECAT programme by McLeod (2011) highlighted the absence of ownership of knowledge and critical reflection within the training programme. It was this lack of pedagogical theory in the ECAT training, of how children acquire language skills, and the lack of time given to reflect on personal assumptions and practice in relation to theory that hindered the impact of the programme. Intuitively, the Communication Project included these elements which enable practitioners to progress from intuitive knowledge towards a much deeper understanding and ownership of knowledge.

As part of this, the project supported the creation of a nursery wide communication environment, embedded high-quality communication strategies and created a reflective learning community of staff and children. It developed a mechanism for providing the opportunity for the staff to continue to develop the nursery's communication and language practice after the conclusion of the project.

The elements: pedagogy into practice

A key element of the project was to harvest the skills, knowledge, and expertise, which constituted the intellectual capital, within the nursery. Intellectual capital is the sum of what everyone in the setting knows and shares that can help the practitioners become more effective in enhancing the learning and development of children. "As the amount of intellectual capital increases, the setting's capacity to add value to the lives of children increases" (Sergiovanni 1992, p 39). Early years settings can only develop intellectual capital when they become enquiring communities, thus there was the need to nurture all practitioners so they had an ambitious vision of what best practice in communication looked like and high expectations of what all children could achieve. Three crucial questions were asked to identify the setting intellectual capital:

- What do we want each child and adult to learn about communication?

- How will we know when each child and adult has learned to communicate?

- How will we respond when a child or adult experiences difficulty in learning to communicate?

It was felt that, prior to the training, there was a lack of confidence and expertise within the setting regarding what adults and children needed to know when working with children who are experiencing challenges with communication. There was a lack of clarity in how managers and practitioners knew how to respond if an adult or child experienced difficulty in learning and staff were often uncertain about what they could do to contribute to the provision of a communication–rich environment.

In addition to the conditions within the nursery, local opportunities to access interdisciplinary training on communication were limited and consisted of a top down approach. The project needed to harness a wider professional background combined with an understanding of early years practice. As Brebner et al. (2016) advocated, successful professional development training requires a multi-disciplinary approach with a professional who understands what early practitioners know and understand about early communication development, and how this relates to the work they do.

Throughout the project it was the chemistry of relationships between professional and practitioner which underpinned the training and development activities. It was felt this approach would result in a more effective collaborative working relationship to meet the communication needs of young children in the setting through developing sustained and enduring good communication practice.

The catalyst: the trainer

Jago and Radford's (2016) research explored speech and language therapists' beliefs around collaborative practice and concluded there were barriers to the transferring of skills between speech and language therapy and early years education. This was deemed to be due to the therapist's role being seen as the provider and receiver of information about a child, but only a provider of skills for practitioners. For true collaboration the mutual transfer of skills and knowledge needs to exist enabling a state of reciprocity to be achieved (Lacey 2001). Having a deep understanding of early years practice, the challenges, the stresses, the excitement and fun, combined with expertise in communication strategies and interventions would provide the chemical reaction needed to create reciprocity within the project.

The trainer commissioned was an early years teacher with a previous early background of working in deprived areas where many of the families spoke English as an additional language (EAL). Consequently, the trainer was acutely aware of the challenges and cognitive advantages afforded bilingual children and the importance of a rich communication environment for successful language acquisition. In addition, for over a decade the focus of the trainer's work had been in Special Educational Needs working with under-fives and their families, designing and delivering training to professionals, and working closely with Speech and Language therapists and early years providers in homes, schools, and settings to support the delivery of appropriate, high-quality learning for all. The trainer was very aware of the chemistry of interagency co-operation and had the deeply held belief that the "best quality services required a holistic approach" (Mroz and Hall 2003, p 118).

The trainer and her colleague's experiences of designing and delivering training demonstrated that, whilst traditional approaches to training showed positive short-term gains for practitioners, there was little evidence that change became embedded across whole settings, and over time could be lost entirely as staff moved on. This resulted in managers accessing the same training packages year after year for their staff.

The trainer's belief grew that training which provided an opportunity for challenge and time for reflection, that promoted honest and non-judgemental discussion, and nurtured relationships, would be most effective in developing the best practice. Therefore, having experienced many years where the chemical formula for training had not resulted in a chain reaction, the trainer relished the opportunity to remix the elements and work in a different way.

I have always enjoyed the dynamics of training, the sharing of thoughts and helping people to work through new ideas together but had found much of training to be of the 'hit and run' variety with too little time allowed for new learning to 'settle' and be tried out.

My job involved a lot of close observation of children's learning and I recognised in them the freedom to rehearse and talk through ideas. I loved how individuals went about the same learning in different ways and the deep satisfaction they had in new achievements and how they built on these achievements with new learning.

Surely this must be a better, more satisfying way to learn?

The crucible: the nursery

Prior to the start of the Project, the nursery manager and senior staff demonstrated a high level of commitment to an honest assessment of staff skills and their engagement levels using the Leuven Scales. These findings provided a baseline for the start of the project against which evaluation could be made. It identified what skills and knowledge practitioners needed to learn and how managers would know they had learnt it. The quality and quantity of spoken language that children hear in interaction with caregivers during the early years of life are important influences on language development (Murray and Egan 2014). However, the practitioners in the setting felt they had little or no training in this area. This lack of training may explain why it had been observed that many of the practitioners did not often use communication facilitating and language modelling strategies which are known to develop children's communication skills.

There was a need for practitioners to embrace the idea of the quality of the communication environment as a significant educator, and to expand that thinking beyond the notion of room arrangements. Practitioners needed to understand the value of creating and sustaining a rich communication environment not only to support the children's communication needs but as a physical reminder of what value they placed on communication.

The Communication Project was rooted in the belief that the way we teach and support learning in young children based on their interests, their learning dispositions, their needs, and their strengths is an effective approach for all learners. It took as a starting point that for learning to be meaningful the learning styles, strengths, and challenges of individuals, their rate of learning and need to rehearse new or revisited skills needed to be acknowledged. It recognised the importance of a trusting, supportive relationship between trainer and learner and between learners themselves as a key component to developing trust and confidence. Learning would become the alchemy, as Vygotsky suggested, when the relationships between the learner and the environment became a complex reciprocal relationship: the "transformation of participation" (Rogoff 1997).

It also drew on elements of Carr's (2001) domains of learning dispositions. The launch of the project fostered an expectation that the project would be interesting and promoted the practitioner's readiness to be involved. This would be elemental in sustaining the project as practitioners would be supported to have the resilience and desire to persist and overcome when difficulties arose, and mistakes were made.

There was a clear need for learners to appreciate colleagues' strengths and to feel that the whole team, from managers to the most recently qualified member of staff, were "in it together" as co-learners. The fear of looking silly or being thought of by others as an inferior practitioner had proved in the past to be a barrier to effective communication between staff and had inhibited confident practice. Staff had felt unable to challenge or compliment the practice of others for fear of losing face. Previously, skills taught in training tended to be seen as something to guard rather than to share and develop. It was essential that this be addressed quickly and simply to ensure that a culture of support and joint enterprise was established at the start.

It felt important to allow practitioners the opportunity to express ideas and feelings to each other as a means of developing their own view of themselves as a communicator. This was rooted in the belief that confident learners, whether they are children or practitioners, are more willing to practise skills, reflect on the outcomes, and adapt accordingly. Indeed, as positive communication experiences and well-being have seen to be linked for children (Law et al. 2017) then cannot the same be true for adults?

Thus the project offered all participants the opportunity to take responsibility in a range of ways, to see another point of view and develop a view of themselves. This was the beginning of a chain reaction, the forming of a new community of learners, indeed an all-embracing learning community.

The chain reaction: project design and delivery

The project differed from other training programmes in many ways. The project design and outcomes were agreed between the manager and trainer and encompassed the knowledge, skills, and practice necessary for the creation of a high-quality communication environment. The first element was to establish a clear vision, with regard to the pedagogy of what and how the adults would learn and a philosophy that the adult–child interaction was central to the project.

The second element was to build the capacity for practitioners to influence each other into action. Explicit attempts were made to design the project in the context of the setting. A quick fix was not an option; the time to meet, discuss, reflect, and train together where chemistry could happen was made a priority. Lewin and Regine (2000) state that it is through relationships that people develop an attachment and a feeling of responsibility, rather than an obligation, towards common goals and objectives and the nature of the training was relational from the outset.

As a practitioner commented:

It has been lovely to see the difference it has made to each other. Although I had worked with a person we didn't really communicate. But being able to be part of something that has purpose, responsibility and is exciting has built our relationship and it has blossomed.

From the start, all staff were given a Project Outline (see Figure 4.1) which detailed the expected outcomes, the description of the areas of training, the expectations placed on all and how the project would be evaluated. This proved an effective method of creating an equality among learners whilst at the same time ensuring a transparency of purpose. It gave a clear reference point throughout the project and meant that all learners and the trainer could be held to account. It indicated a level of mutual trust and respect irrespective of the role or status of the participant. By designing this flexible and thus reflective approach to training, it was possible to mirror the plan and review models common to early years practice ensuring an accurately targeted and successful programme of learning.

The Project Launch

The Project Launch was a key event, deliberately celebratory in tone with cake and a range of engaging activities with staff able to join in and work together. In addition the Launch began to nurture trust in existing staff relationships creating an atmosphere in nursery where staff were able to value and voice their appreciation of what individual members of the community brought to the whole.

It acted as a springboard for what was to follow and took place one evening for an hour and a half at the end of the nursery day with all staff required to attend. It was designed to inform, enthuse, engage, involve, and inspire.

The Launch enabled the trainer to establish an early rapport and express her availability to individuals for questions and comments at agreed times during later visits throughout the project and thereafter by email.

The Launch gave the trainer the opportunity, by using carefully designed activities, to learn about individuals' understanding of communication and give a general snapshot of their ease at using language.

ACTIVITIES

- Each participant introduced their neighbour and said one thing which they admired about their practice. In the event, it proved to be an unexpectedly moving experience for many which continued after the session into the following week when several members of staff expressed to the manager how no one had ever said positive things about their practice before and how good that made them feel.

- Each participant was required to take a strawberry in turn, taste it, and choose an adjective to describe it. Individuals were asked to think of a word that had not been used before. This activity provided a crude but early indicator of possible restricted adult vocabulary which could suggest limitations to the provision of a rich language experience for the children. This helped the trainer to target training specifically rather than generically.

Continuing the project

Room and individual observations and whole nursery training took place over the following weeks; the trainer was able to spend time with groups and individuals to revisit learning, provide one to one or small group coaching, model practice with children and to carry out observations as and when the need was apparent. Practical support was given to establish effective and engaging communication environments.

This varied and dynamic approach to training proved successful in no small part because of the commitment to building trusting, relaxed and non-judgemental relationships across the nursery, reflecting Bennett et al.'s (2003, p 9) belief that "teams operate best in an open climate, with relations based on mutual trust and open communication in a supportive organisational climate".

A practitioner commented:

It has been interesting how as a team we have often had the same thoughts and ideas and agree how to do things. It has given us all confidence on how we think as a team. It has made a real difference to the teaching and learning and the children.

A significant area of development for staff at the nursery was the expectation that they would be involved in peer to peer observations. Whilst this was a big ask for staff, being able to work, communicate, and learn collaboratively included the willingness to hold themselves and each other to account. This was a key and necessary aspect of the whole community's ability to move forward and consolidate positive changes.

Positive relationships as a catalyst for confident and reflective learners was a "golden thread" which was woven throughout the project mirroring the "companionable learning ... whereby well-being develops" (Roberts 2010, p 53). Thus, within the project a discreet training module was designed by the trainer developing the strengths observed in individuals or groups and leaning heavily, in the first instance, on noticing, and being able to comment on, good practice. This was extended, in small steps, to support staff in making constructive comments on aspects of the observation that they felt could be improved and whether they could play a supportive role in that improvement. Initially the Communication Room Leads practised these skills in their own groups and their findings and feedback were moderated in a training session with the trainer. This was then rolled out to all staff, with managers and leads taking on the role of support and moderation.

Whole group training was also carried out on specific or more specialised communication subjects such as working with children who had English as an Additional Language and it was always followed-up practically, in ways that staff had indicated they would find most helpful. This required flexibility because practitioners for different age groups needed support in different ways. This meant that training needed to be dynamic and responsive, once more reflecting back good quality and effective nursery practice.

As one early years practitioner stated:

Doing it in little stages gives you time to practise a little and embed it before you move to the next stage. You can reflect on which bits worked. If we hadn't

*had time to reflect and trial things it would have been quite demoralising –
you think you have a long way to go, but we did a little bit at a time and people started to embrace it.*

Some training was specifically for the Setting Communication Lead Person,
appointed to work with the manager and trainer, and the Room Communication
Leads who had responsibility to support, engage, and ensure information was
shared and tasks completed. This group worked closely together to explore ways
that they could best share information with colleagues, make practical changes,
encourage the staff in their room, and work to have consistently excellent communication practice across the nursery.

As one Communication Room Leader commented:

*Some staff approach me and say,' I'm a bit unsure, can you advise me?' They
haven't been embarrassed – if they say will you help me, that's fine – they're
not afraid to talk to you now about it.*

In no small part, this group of room leaders became fundamental to the ongoing
success of the project, demonstrating cooperative working and positive relationships. This distributive leadership model called for a shift away from the "traditional vision of the leader being one key individual towards a more collective
vision, one where the responsibility for leadership rests with both formal and
informal leaders" (Siraj-Blatchford and Manni 2007, p 19). The project enabled
people and ideas to bounce off each other, combining elements in a different way
creating a "new field" in communication training.

Outcomes: reaching critical mass, a new community of practice

In summary, the project took well-researched and proven ideas of what separate
elements constitute excellent practice using familiar strategies for supporting effective communication and acknowledging how a rich and deeply engaging communication environment can nurture children's well-being and development. However,
it also recognised that in order for these separate elements to have an enduring
impact on practice and outcomes, they needed to come together in an innovative
way to create a whole that was of far greater significance than its individual parts.

This alchemy was created by regarding the nursery as a community of practice
(Wenger 2011) where the learning of all, from the most to the least experienced
practitioner, was explicitly acknowledged as important. The Communication

Project created a culture where practitioners knew their skills to be valued and took pleasure in companionable learning by finding excitement and satisfaction in experiencing the impact that learning had on their own self-esteem and that of their colleagues. In turn the confidence to try new approaches with the children and suggest and implement changes to enhance the nursery environment resulted in very obvious delight and professional satisfaction as children's eagerness, enjoyment, and willingness to communicate grew.

In the same way that no practitioner was left to flounder with learning something that they had found difficult to understand but had someone to work alongside them to support their learning, practitioners worked together reflectively to find ways to support the learning of all children. They demonstrated that they were more skilled at noticing and reflecting on a child's interests and *how* they learned, rather than just observing *what* they were doing. This was clearly reflected in their written observations and contributions to children's learning journeys. Because practitioners were being noticed and encouraged as valuable and valued members of the learning community, they were more able to see the children as fellow learners and relationships between adults and children were enriched.

By valuing all learners, including managers, trainer, and practitioners, and understanding and embracing the currency of positive relationships in this shared Communication Project, the nursery community was able to flourish, and a flourishing community provides rich opportunity for children to flourish too.

Three years on...

It has been very satisfying to go back and visit the nursery from time to time. Staff are keen to show me their rooms and the physical improvements they have made to the learning environment that have come as a direct result of their own learning and improved understanding. On occasion they ask about the finer points of some aspect of communication which is fine. It has been great to see how confident they are and although it is hard to quantify and measure, there really does feel to be a more relaxed, and happy atmosphere in the nursery.

Sue Hobson – Trainer

True success must rest on whether the impact of any training becomes embedded in practice and is sustainable. With the Communication Project not only was the objective to improve knowledge, understanding, and practice with regards to communication but to effect a change in the culture of the nursery.

Seeing themselves as continuing learners, and hence an integral part of a larger learning community, has allowed a level of openness to change which would have been very difficult to envisage prior to the start of the project. This openness to new ideas and the willingness to engage in discussion has meant that they can be shared, and changes agreed.

It is interesting to note that practitioners' own awareness and improvement in communication skills has resulted in more meaningful observations of the children. Personal awareness has led to a greater awareness of what the children are communicating through their choices, their body language, their manner of play, and their words. This has enabled practitioners to provide a learning environment more fitted to the developing needs of individual children and mirrors the approach taken to their own learning. Children's communication with adults and each other is consistently supported and encouraged and this has resulted in improved relationships throughout the community.

Practitioners demonstrate greater willingness and creativity in their approach planning for children's learning and provided richer learning opportunities for all. The community shows a shared delight in new achievements and it is commonplace to hear staff share and celebrate success.

On a more practical level, there is an expectation that visual systems are in place and used across the nursery in an age and stage appropriate way and all new and temporary members of staff are supported to use them so that there is a coherent approach to communication practice through the provision of an enabling environment.

On occasion practitioners email the trainer for clarification of a point of practice or to share something they are trying which promotes an ongoing commitment to excellent and up to date practice.

Key to this success is the manager's desire for the development of her staff, her willingness to listen to them and allow time for discussion and training and her unwavering and enduring passion for the development and education of the little children in her care.

Distinctive threads throughout the project

- The firm belief that the principles, processes, and practices clearly laid out in the EYFS are equally applicable to adult learning.

- Deliberate emphasis on building positive relationships as a key to nurturing confident and skilled practitioners.

- A close working relationship between manager and trainer.

- A clear model of distributed leadership by the manager.

- A common aim understood by all with a commitment to and expectation of success.

- An early focus on creating high expectations of commitment from all staff and the trainer.

- Training opportunities which supported the development of positive staff relationships.

- Flexible and timely delivery responsive to group or individual needs as they became apparent.

- A designated Communication Lead Person with a lead person for each age group with allocated time to meet for training and discussion and an ongoing role and responsibility beyond the end of the project.

- Specific training for all staff on Positive Peer Observations and feedback methods.

- Opportunities to name and celebrate success.

PROVOCATIONS

- Look at the list of distinctive threads throughout the project and identify the differences that you find between the project approach and the traditional approaches to training.

- What would you identify as the main gains from this approach?

- What might be the barriers to success of this approach and how might you overcome them?

- Both manager and trainer acknowledge that parents are a crucial part of any nursery community and yet they are not part of this project. Why do you think this might be and how could you develop that aspect of work using this project model?

References

Bennett, N., Wise, C., Wood, P., and Harvey, J., 2003. *Distributive leadership: A literature review.* London: NCSL. Available at: http://oro.open.ac.uk/8534/1/bennett-distributed-leadership-full.pdf [Accessed 17. 06.2018].

Brebner, C., Jovanovic, J., Lawless, A., and Young, J., 2016. Early childhood educators' understanding of communication: Application to their work with young children. *Child Language Teaching and Therapy,* 32 (3), 277–292.

Carr, M. 2001. *Assessments in early childhood setting: Learning stories.* London: SAGE.

Coburn, C.E., 2003. Rethinking scale: Moving beyond numbers to deep and lasting change. *Educational Researcher*, 32 (3), 3–12.

Department for Children, Schools and Families, 2008. Every child a talker. https://www.foundationyears.org.uk/files/2011/10/ecat_guidance_for_practitioners_31.pdf. [Accessed 1.11.18].

Department for Education, 2017. *Early Years Foundation Stage Statutory Framework (EYFS)* Available at: https://www.gov.uk/government/publications/early-years-foundation-stage-framework--2 [Accessed 27.03.2018].

Jago, S., and Radford, J. 2016. SLT beliefs about collaborative practice: Implications for education and learning. *Child Language Teaching and Therapy*, 33 (2), 199–213.

Jopling, M., Whitmarsh, J., and Hadfield, M., 2013. The challenges of evaluation: Assessing Early Talk's impact on speech language and communication practise in children's centres. *International Journal of Early Years Education*, 21 (1), 70–84.

Lacey, P., 2001. *Support partnerships: Collaboration in action.* London: David Fulton.

Law, J., Charlton, J., and Asmussen, K., 2017. *Language as a child well-being indicator.* London: Early Intervention Foundation.

Lewin, R., and Regine, B., 2000. *The soul at work.* New York: Simon & Schuster.

McDonald, D., Proctor, P., Gill, W., Heaven, S., Marr, J., and Young, J., 2015. Increasing early childhood educator's use of communication-facilitating and language-modelling strategies: Brief speech and language therapy training. *Child Language Teaching and Therapy*, 31 (3), 1–18.

McLeod, N. 2011. Exploring early years educators' ownership of language and communication knowledge and skills: A review of key policy and initial reflections on Every Child a Talker and its implementation. *Education*, 39 (4), 3–13, 429–445.

Mroz, M. and Hall, E. 2003. Not yet identified: The knowledge, skills and training needs of early years professionals in relation to children's speech and language development. *Early Years*, 23 (2), 117–130.

Murray, A. and Egan, S. 2014. Does reading to infants benefit their cognitive development at 9-months old? An investigation using a large birth cohort survey. *Child Language Teaching and Therapy*, 31 (3), 305–322.

Office for Standards in Education (Ofsted), 2015. *Early years inspection handbook 2015.* Available at: www.gov.uk/goverment/organisation/ofsted [Accessed 20.09. 2018].

Roberts, R., 2010. *Wellbeing from birth.* London: Sage.

Rogoff, B., 1997. Evaluating development in the process of participation. In *Theory, methods, and practice building on each other. Ch 13 in Change and Development: Issues of Theory, Method, and Application*, edited by Amsel, E. and Renninger, K. A. Mahwah, NJ: Lawrence Erlbaum Associates.

Sergiovanni, T., 1992. *Moral leadership: Getting to the heart of school improvement.* San Francisco: Jossey-Bass.

Siraj-Blatchford, I., and Manni, L., 2007. *Effective leadership in the early years sector. The ELEYS study.* London: Institute of Education, University of London.

Tickell, C., 2011. *The early years: Foundations for life, health and learning – An independent report on the early years foundation stage to Her Majesty's government.* Great Britain: DfE.

Wenger, E., 2011. Communities of practice: A brief introduction. https://scholarsbank.uoregon.edu/xmlui/handle/1794/11736 [Accessed 1.11.2018].

Collaborative practice in communication for the early years

The learning from a research project

Julie Kent and Sarah McDonald

OVERVIEW OF CHAPTER

Research into the communication environment and the knowledge and skills of early years practitioners suggests a significant degree of variation in the quality of the communication environment encountered by children in early years settings. This chapter examines the findings from research into an approach to staff development in this area in Nottinghamshire where the Speech and Language Therapy team have worked closely with setting staff to develop the role of the Language Lead within settings across the county as part of a commissioned universal service. The chapter will present an understanding of good practice in this collaborative context and will consider what the research findings suggest for the wider public health agenda in the area of children's communication needs, bringing it back to the practitioner and the learning environment for both the practitioner and the child.

In the UK, the government estimates that there are 3.1 million Ofsted registered childcare places (Department for Education 2017a), 53% of these being school-based, 39% being group-based, and the remaining 9% being registered childminder places. Latest data (Department for Education 2018) suggests a 90% take-up of the offer of 30 hours' free childcare for 3-year-olds and, although the uptake for funded 2-year-old places is less, with potentially several million children attending early years (EY) settings during the day, it is clear that these settings play a substantial role in determining what and how children will learn and develop. Research and practice evidence suggests that a child's communication and language skills and any early difficulties in this area can be a determining factor in their long-term life chances (Law et al. 2017).

However, research into the communication environment and the knowledge and skills of EY practitioners suggests a significant degree of variation in the quality of the communication environments encountered by children in EY settings. Most staff working in EY settings have received limited or no specific additional training around children's language and communication needs (Mroz and Hall 2003). Given the amount of time children spend in these settings, and the crucial stage in language development at which these settings are accessed, this poses significant questions about the quality of the environments and language-learning opportunities that children are typically experiencing.

Since Mroz & Hall's research (2003), there has been a considerable investment by government in continuing professional development (CPD) for EY staff around communication and language in the early years including Every Child A Talker (ECAT) and its younger "sibling" The Early Language Development Programme (ELDP). The implication was that these cascade models of training for EY staff were an efficient and effective way of managing children's Speech, Language and Communication Needs (SLCN), particularly in the early years, fitting with the preferred early intervention model espoused by successive governments since New Labour's SureStart programme was instigated in the early 2000s. In response to the Bercow review (Bercow 2008), The Communication Trust was also established as a body which would champion Speech, Language and Communication (SLC) across disciplines with a focus on research and evidence-based practice. These high profile and large-scale national actions show that there was recognition of the potential to address children's communication needs within EY settings. In addition, in many areas of the country there have been a number of joint commissioning initiatives in the public health sphere between local authorities and health trusts to support the ongoing delivery of Speech and Language Therapy (SLT) and workforce development initiatives in EY settings.

However, this investment in SLT services has waned in the face of national austerity, Local Authority (LA) budget cuts, and changes to service provision. In 2017, The Communication Trust had its annual grant from the Department of Education withdrawn. This is despite the fact that, although the Foundation Stage Profiles for Communication and Language have shown some broad improvements (Department for Education 2017b), there continue to be a number of concerns, in particular for the persistent gender gap between boys and girls in this prime area of learning and also the performance for the most disadvantaged groups continuing to be depressed in relation to peers. As highlighted in Farley and Hobson's chapter, there remains a significant gap in the knowledge and skills possessed by EY staff in relation to children's communication.

In addition, in her evaluation of the ECAT programme and its effectiveness, McLeod (2011), while recognising the crucial necessity for skilled carers and educators facilitated by high-quality training, suggests that there have been inherent difficulties with the cascade model of practitioner training. In particular she focusses on the ownership of knowledge by the early years practitioners involved as recipients of the training and notes that, for the learning to be effectively implemented and embedded into the setting practice, there is a need to support practitioner reflection on and application of the knowledge and skills to "progress from intuitive knowledge towards a much deeper, more meaningful system of professional understandings and ownership" (ibid., p430).

Speech and Language Therapy (SLT) services for children are typically seen as the appropriate providers of the training required for the needs of children with SLCN. The Royal College of Speech and Language Therapists (RCSLT) details the role of the SLT in supporting the delivery of public health to children and notes the importance of making health commissioners aware of the evidence base around the efficacy of SLT as well as the value of early intervention and working alongside education providers, particularly in EY provisions. There is an evidence-based need for a strong commissioning strategy for SLT community services for early intervention and joint commissioning of services has been central to the development of good integrated practice in parts of the country where this approach has been implemented (ICAN 2018).

However, the capacity of these services is limited and there is a very varied picture of service delivery and commissioning strategy across the country resulting in a post-code disparity of SLT provision. In the 2018 review 10 years on from the original Bercow review of SLT provision (ICAN 2018), it is apparent that local disparities in service provision remain, being based on available resources rather than need and that commissioning of SLT services is still not equitable or consistently managed. However, there is a strong case for early intervention, in line with a public health model. Public Health England identified children's early communication and language development as central to school readiness (PHE 2016) and SLC has been recognised increasingly as a public health issue, particularly since the move in responsibility for commissioning SLT services to Local Authorities from October 2015. Part of this new model has resulted in attempts to coordinate the EYFS 2-year progress check with the Healthy Child Programme 2-year health and development review (Dept for Education 2014). However, this integrated 2-year review, although resulting in some improved collaboration and better working relationships between health and EY staff, has proved problematic to implement consistently and has highlighted the variation in judgements and assessments around SLCN between different practitioners. Yet, in financial terms alone, there is good evidence that investment in SLCN as a public health issue provides a good return in relation to school readiness and long-term educational progression (City of Stoke 2017). Bercow suggests that crucially, "Understanding of speech, language and communication should be embedded in initial qualifications and continuing professional development for all relevant practitioners" (ICAN 2018, p31).

If all EY settings were able to provide environments that more actively facilitated communication, and if all EY staff had specific training to support them to address the communication needs of children, this would not only reduce the pressure on SLT services but, more importantly, would potentially reduce the number of children who go on to develop SLCN. This issue is specifically considered in Farley and Hobson's chapter in their case history discussion of an innovative training approach in a single setting.

Law and Pagnamenta (2017), in their discussion around communication as a public health concern, identify the training of a "communication champion" in a setting as a key universal intervention in the area. This can be achieved through SLT services working collaboratively with EY settings to train staff in these settings. Often, this involves training staff to identify and work with children with SLCN (ibid.). This might be through specific guidance and provision of programmes for an individual child, which are monitored and updated by the SLT or through generic training provided to a whole setting or key setting staff on a "need to know" basis.

The response to needs in Nottinghamshire

At the start of the aforementioned ECAT programme, the Nottinghamshire Child and Family Partnership SLT service (NCFP SLT) also started a programme which they called the Language Lead (LL) Approach. In this approach, individual practitioners working in foundation units in schools and in early years settings are recruited to act as the LL for the setting, which involves taking responsibility for promoting communication within the setting. These staff work with a local SLT through a stepped programme of training and support moving beyond the cascade model, which can be accessed at a universal level and is aimed at developing and supporting the role of a Language Lead identified as a champion for SLC issues within an EY setting.

By early 2017, over 150 LLs were active in Nottinghamshire, being supported by a small core team of community SLTs. An evidence base for this approach was sought as the NCFP SLT service wished to find out:

1. how the implementation of the LL approach was experienced by SLTs, LLs, and the managers of EY settings;
2. how effective the LL approach was perceived as being by SLTs, LLs, and the managers of EY settings;
3. what could be done to improve upon the implementation and effectiveness of the LL approach, and what strengths of the LL approach could be identified and shared more widely.

Independent researchers from Nottingham Trent University were asked to explore through interviews the questions posed above. 9 SLTs, 16 LLs, and 9 EY settings managers were interviewed in 2017 and their responses were analysed thematically, guided by the Consolidated Framework for Implementation Research (CFIR) (Damschroder et al. 2009). The findings from the research pertinent to this chapter will be explored below.

As a result of examining the research findings it is also possible to identify key aspects of good practice in the current context and to consider what the research findings suggest for the wider public health agenda and the leadership of learning in the area of communication.

Main findings from the research

A valued and needed approach.

There was strong evidence of belief in the LLs about increasing needs in children's SLC and most LLs interviewed believed that children in their particular area had higher SLC needs than average. This echoes the growing awareness already identified here and elsewhere about the SLC issues in the population.

Across the spectrum of practitioners involved it was clear that the LL approach to working with SLCN was positively received. The approach was seen as good practice by SLTs and LLs alike and SLTs reported evidence of improved practice where the LL approach was implemented:

> *You ask them to do an environmental audit, and the next time you come into the setting, it's, there's been change, so there's, so you know there's tents and tepees and there's, you know they've changed the resources they have in the mud kitchen because they've thought about how they can expand the language there, but it's just, for me the, always the most visual thing anyway is the change in the physical environment and setting.*

LLs expressed improved confidence in their knowledge when discussing a child's communication needs with parents, thus having an impact in the child's mesosystem:

> *Parents will ask you what can I do ... so I suppose in that sense you've expanded your knowledge and your ideas that you can pass on to parents and strategies ... so I have learnt quite a lot from being the LL.*

An unsystematic introduction

A number of LLs discussed how they experienced the initial introduction to the role as being rather haphazard and noted that they were uncertain about the process of selection to be a LL. Whilst some felt pleased to be "chosen", the notion of being selected to be the LL was not seen positively by all the LLs. As one LL stated:

> when I first started I don't think anybody had a clue of what they were expecting from us … I certainly didn't know what they were expecting from me … it was a piece, a label on a piece of paper that I'd got, that we'd got to put down, Ofsted purposes.

SLTs also noted how LLs were often given the role by a setting manager without a clear strategy:

> It just seems to be whoever is available in the setting to do it. Sometimes I meet people and they're really keen and they've wanted to do it for ages … in others (settings) it feels like they've just been given the role. They might be the SENCo and the LL and everything extra is just shoved on them.

An adaptable approach

The research found a degree of flexibility in the way the LL approach was implemented, a feature that was also valued by the LLs and the SLTs. It was clearly apparent that different LLs interpret and apply the role quite differently depending on the setting and the needs of the children. For some this became a monitoring role, tracking the progress of individual children and referring to targeted services when required, whereas for others, change has involved them taking on the responsibility for "delivering" language groups for targeted children. Still others have focussed on developing their role in changing the setting environment to be more communication friendly. However, in all cases LLs have noted how, to some extent, they have changed their own personal practice in the way that they talk and listen to all children, employing universal communication strategies and demonstrating a recognition of the centrality of communication and language in supporting all areas of children's learning and development:

> It's so easy to change your interactions, you know even alter them slightly and to have it at the heart of what you do, because especially in early years you know it's not all about writing … it's about that communication and that's for every area of learning down there, the communication underpins it all.

An approach which builds on practitioner knowledge

The Early Years Foundation Stage (EYFS) (DfE 2017c.) has very clear guidance for practitioners in providing an enabling environment to support early C&L development and the intention of the LL model was to build on EY practitioner's understanding in this area. The LL approach supports the development of an identified practitioner in a setting who would take the lead in developing this aspect of the setting offer and disseminate their own learning in championing language and communication throughout the setting having been supported by an SLT and the tools, structure, and training framework which was provided around the approach. The relevance of the approach is summed up below by this LL in a Foundation Unit:

> *It is such a crucial part of what we have to do on a day to day basis, you know urm, we really do value talk, and we really do value children's talk, and, urm, I just think, I don't know, it's just so vitally important isn't it you can tell, we get a lot of children come in and they're just at such a disadvantage you know they've not had you know even if it's just those singing songs and reading stories with the parents and you know actually having conversations or, you know being listened to and being given time to talk that urm, and for me I love learning, you know what I mean, it was an opportunity for me to do some I suppose some self-education if you like, you know, and just going out and seeking that opportunity, but you know it's just it's just lovely whatever you get from the network and being able to bring it back into school and being able to share it with the rest of the staff team and things like that, I don't know it just appealed to me, its sits really well with what, with what we are, are trying to do in our ethos and our school environment so it didn't take any selling at all, it was just like well yeah this sounds wonderful, and it's fantastic having the network meetings and being able to go and talk to other people and share ideas and you know a bit of self-reflection time if anything you know, getting out and you know thinking about things and urm trying to come back to school and put it into, put into, into plan.*

This practitioner valued the approach for the children in the setting but also for herself as a learner and communicator and the cycle of development is clearly seen here.

Similarly, the SLT viewpoint here echoes these feelings about the importance of having a communication champion in the EY setting:

> *So, I normally describe it as, 'You're the champion for language in your setting. You're the one who makes sure it's always on everybody's agenda, so if*

> *you're planning or you're in a team meeting, you're the person who says,*
> *"What about language?" Also, you don't have to have all the answers. You're*
> *the link person, so it's okay to say, "I haven't got a clue, but I can go and*
> *ring the speech therapist and find out for you". You're the person who knows*
> *about referrals, but again, you don't have to know. It's okay to go and ring.*
> *"I know someone in another setting who I've met at network. I can go and*
> *talk to them and we'll figure it out. I can go and talk to the SENCO". So, you're*
> *the champion in your setting.*

Leadership for language: practitioner development

Of great interest to the researchers and pertinent to current debate around practitioner qualifications was the view of SLTs that the success of the LL approach
was highly dependent on the leadership qualities and competencies of the LL
and the degree of autonomy that they were given to execute their role. This was
seen by participants from both groups, but particularly the SLTs, to be highly
dependent on the overall setting management and the gatekeeper role of the setting manager. LLs also identified the need for the approach to be embraced by
colleagues across the setting as well as by management in order for it to become
part of setting practice:

> *at the end of the day, it comes down to the people working in the room, you*
> *know, the teachers and the TAs, they've all got to be really on board, and get*
> *it, and if they don't, and it, you know it doesn't fit with what their style is, it's*
> *just, I won't say it's impossible because it isn't but that is the biggest barrier.*

This clearly has implications for practice in communication and language in
EY settings and also for the dissemination of knowledge beyond the Foundation
Stage. Most LLs expressed concern that SLC needs, whilst increasing, were not
being addressed beyond the Foundation years and that the LL approach was generally confined to the Foundation stage in their settings where they were working
in a primary school setting.

Development Matters states that "Children learn and develop well in enabling
environments, in which their experiences respond to their individual needs
(and there is a strong partnership between practitioners and parents and carers)"
(Early Education 2017, p2). Early years pedagogy, grounded in the EYFS principles, embraces the centrality of the enabling environment in supporting learning and development as settings seek to "value all people" and "value learning"
(ibid., p2). This piece of research identified how the successful implementation

of an approach to developing an enabling environment for children as part of a whole setting communication strategy was significantly influenced by the leadership capacity of the individuals involved.

Leadership is pivotal in the development of communication within a setting. The concept of pedagogical leadership, "forms of practice that shape and form teaching and learning" (Male and Palaiolgou 2013, p214), is likely to be a key factor in the success or otherwise of this model of working. Where leadership is developed and distributed across the staff team to enable and empower, good practice can be developed and there was evidence that this was facilitated by the structure of the LL approach. Themes common to the early years practice of "having a go", support for risk-taking and exploration, and "deep involvement" (Laevers 2005), were raised in the interview as the learning and development of LLs echoed the characteristics of effective learning:

> It was quite daunting because erm I was, I also went to just the early years network meetings and because I felt slightly out of my depth because of having not taught nursery before I was just trying to glean as much information from people around me and from things that I was being offered, erm, so it was a little bit daunting, and so for the first few sessions you sort of sit back and think what are they talking about? But then then the penny starts to drop and you start to see things in your setting that you think yeh no, that's that, you know, that's a child doing that kind of approach, and I think it was the second year that I did the courses, which of course then it just became so obvious, cos I'd had a whole year in nursery seeing all this, and I though yeh I can relate to that, and then the training obviously gave me the confidence to think yeh I know what I'm talking about (laughs).

This training and support model to develop EY practitioners in the LL approach also has parallels with the associated move in the EY field to develop and improve the knowledge, skills, and qualifications of EY practitioners. Within the set of graduate skills for EY practitioners, the nine graduate practitioner competencies includes "Collaborating with others" as a key competency for EY professionals (Early Childhood Studies Degrees Network [ECSDN] 2018).

Reflecting on the research findings, the fact that the research process has identified as one of its themes the need for developing leadership capacity in EY teams has resulted in the recognition that there is a mismatch of expectation and understanding between those devising, planning, and promoting the service and the expectations and understanding of those participating in the collaborative delivery model. Research by Jago and Radford (2016) concludes that, although there is a mixed range of experience in SLTs in relation to their training in this area, SLTs value and expect a degree of collaboration between their service and EY practitioners when working with children in EY settings and this project confirmed these findings. The research in Nottinghamshire shows a similar level of expectation from NHS SLTs offering the support and training to develop a LL within a local setting, viewing this as a positive and proactive approach to universal delivery of SLT services. However, one of the findings from the research in discussion with nominated LLs was their suspicion that their role had been put in place as a response to service cuts within the SLT service and there was a suggestion that they were possibly being used to fill a gap in service provision. Conversely, the SLT team saw this very much as a key role within a setting with strong personal development opportunities for both the setting and the individual in order to improve the environment and outcomes for the child. Here was clearly where communication and language as a public health concern and as a prime area of learning could be aligned to support the same outcomes for the child where health and education meet.

Possible barriers and challenges to effective collaboration within the child's ecological system

The relationships operating in the child's mesosystem between settings and the SLT service inevitably produce some issues of interpretation of the approach. Because of these different perspectives, the research identified some differing views about what might be a barrier to effectively collaborating to support children's SLC development. Payler and Georgeson's (2013) study on interagency working notes aspects of confidence and communication as being central to facilitating strong interagency working and this aspect was echoed in the Nottinghamshire study with both SLTs and EY practitioners commenting on their own (and other's) levels of confidence in working using the LL model. The type of setting was also identified as having an impact on the quality of practitioner communication practice and this links to the aspects noted by some SLTs around the successful implementation of the LL approach and the practical difficulties in continuity of practice in, for example, pack-away preschools. The frequency of changes to the staff team in EY settings was identified by several SLTs as a barrier to maintaining and developing consistently good practice. Conversely, Payler and Georgson (ibid.) suggest that there can be a lack of understanding by other professionals of contemporary preschool practice but this was not apparent in the LL study as SLTs demonstrated a very good awareness of the current EYFS framework for example, and made use of this as a tool to develop discussion around C&L provision in the settings. SLTs also demonstrated a good deal of empathy in relation to the demands on practitioners in EY settings and there was evidence of effective collaborative relationships on both sides.

Bradford (2012, p43) notes that members of a team need "to understand the nature of collaborative practice" and that early years working is "people-based; highly dependent on interpersonal relationships and shared values". This fits with the early years perspective on learning that suggest that learning takes place within the context of positive relationships, an enabling environment, and where the needs of the unique learner are recognised and built on. Some practitioners described difficulties in the implementation of the approach at a micro level which were linked to the levels of influence that the LL can have either on the beliefs and behaviours of other staff and/or the environment and change within it.

At the macro level this research clearly presents a challenge to those Higher Education Institutions involved in the training of SLTs. A number of SLTs in this study expressed that their clinical training had not prepared them for the way their public health role would operate within the LL approach. If the public health model continues to be shown to be an effective and relevant way of working, particularly in the current climate of large and expanding caseloads and small staff teams, then SLTs should receive training in this way of working.

I don't think we learn that when we train, that kind of advisory capacity that we're all being encouraged to go into.

A key reflection point for the SLT team as result of this research was that training which is "delivered", either 1:1 or through the LL networks needs to be underpinned by a pedagogical approach which understands the need for the conditions for active learning, persistence, and engagement as well as critical thinking which interrogates practice and informs succession planning and capacity building within the workforce. Harris and Lambert (2003) highlight the importance of certain conditions to be in place before capacity for improving practice can occur. To create leadership capacity and opportunities for people within a setting to work together in new ways, there need to be two essential conditions which are the capacity within the setting to manage change and sustain improvements as well as effective reciprocal relationships between the participants.

This research has highlighted the issue of what contributes to effective change in practice in developing the enabling environment, whether this particular approach has been effective and what has made it so in comparison with previous and similar projects. "When goals are clear, feedback relevant and challenges and skill are in balance, attention becomes ordered and fully invested" (Csikszentmihalyi 2009, p32). These themes echo through the learning and development of the LL practitioner in understanding and using the communication strategies in order to effectively implement the LL approach. The sense of persisting with uncertainty and challenge, supported by scaffolding provided by the SLT was clear in many of the interview themes.

Concluding points

In their final report to the NCFP SLT service, the researchers noted that "If the public health model continues to be shown to be an effective and relevant way of working, particularly in the current climate of large and expanding caseloads and small staff teams, then SLTs should receive training in this way of working". By implication, this demands that this and other good practice models used should continue to be standardised and evaluated.

The learning dispositions of staff need to be valued and considered in the construction, development, and delivery of the LL approach in the same way that EY practitioners plan, deliver, observe, and reflect in their planning cycle when working with the learning and development of young children. (EYFS 2017).

Male and Palaiologou (2013) suggest that concepts of "effectiveness" which tend to dominate success measures do not take into account the centrality of relationships and the interactive nature of learner engagement. They use the concept of praxis and consider that the influence of the environment and the community is central to any project that looks to benefit more than just the individual. That is, the results are more than just a sum of the parts. This approach can be applied to the establishment of core or shared values which are embraced by the team within a setting in response to the LL programme.

PROVOCATIONS

- Does considering SLCN as a public health issue alter your perspectives on communication and language as a prime area of learning and development? How?

- Who is responsible for the SLCN of the child in an EY setting and what might this involve for a child with SLCN?

- Do all staff feel confident in implementing and supporting an enabling communication environment?

- What are the leadership qualities required in EY practitioners to act as a language champion in the setting and what might be the barriers to achieving this?

References

Bercow, J. 2008. *The Bercow report: A review of services for children and young people (0–19) with speech, language and communication needs.* Nottingham: DCSF.

Bradford, H., 2012. *The wellbeing of children under three.* Oxon: Routledge.

City of Stoke. 2017. *Early communication impact Report.* Stoke on Trent: City of Stoke LA.

Csikszentmihalyi, M., 2009. *Flow: The psychology of optimal experience.* London: Harper Perennial.

Damschroder, L. J. et al., 2009. Fostering implementation of health services research findings into practice: a consolidated framework for advancing implementation science. *Implementation Science.* 4 (50).

Department for Education, 2017a. *Childcare and early years providers survey: 2016. Statistics on the characteristics of early years providers in England.* Great Britain.

Department for Education, 2017b. *Early years foundation stage profile results in England.* Available at: https://assets.publishing.service.gov.uk/government/uploads/system/uploads/attachment_data/file/652602/SFR60_2017_Text.pdf [Accessed 29.9.18].

Department for Education, 2017c. *Early years foundation stage statutory framework (EYFS)* Available at: https://www.gov.uk/government/publications/early-years-foundation-stage-framework--2 [Accessed 27.03.2018].

Departmentt for Education, 2018. *30 hours free childcare, England, summer term 2018. (Experimental statistics).* Available at: https://assets.publishing.service.gov.uk/government/uploads/system/uploads/attachment_data/file/717709/30HoursFreeChildcareSummerTerm2018Text.pdf [Accessed 29.09.18].

Early Education, 2012. *Development matters in the early years foundation stage (EYFS).* London: Early Education.

ECSDN, 2018. *Striving for excellence: Early childhood graduate practitioner competencies.* Newcastle upon Tyne: ECSDN.

Harris, A. and Lambert, L., 2003. *Building leadership capacity for school improvement.* Maidenhead: Open University Press.

ICAN. 2018. *Bercow ten years on: An independent review of provision for children and young people with speech, language and communication needs in England.* London: ICAN.

Jago, S. and Radford, J., 2016. SLT beliefs about collaborative practice: Implications for education and learning. *Child Language Teaching and Therapy.* 33 (2), 199–213.

Laevers, F., ed., 2005. *Well-being and involvement in care A process-oriented self-evaluation instrument for care setting.* Leuven: Kind & Gezin and Research Centre for Experiential Education

Law, J. and Pagnamenta, E., 2017. Promoting the development of young children's language. *RCSLT Bulletin* (January p12–15). RCSLT: London.

Law, J. et al., 2017. *Early language development: Needs, provision, and intervention for preschool children from socio-economically disadvantaged backgrounds. A report for the education endowment foundation.* UK: EEF.

Male, T. and Palaiolgou, I., 2013. Pedagogical leadership in the 21st century: Evidence from the field. *Educational Management, Administration and Leadership.* 43 (2), 214–231.

McLeod, N. 2011. Exploring early years educators' ownership of language and communication knowledge and skills: a review of key policy and initial reflections on Every Child a Talker and its implementation. *Education.* 39 (4), 3–13, 429–445.

Mroz, M. and Hall, E., 2003. Not yet identified: The knowledge, skills and training needs of early years professionals in relation to children's speech and language development. *Early Years: An International Journal of Research and Development.* 23 (2), 117–130.

Payler, J. and Georgeson, J., 2013. Multiagency working in the early years: confidence, competence and context, *Early Years.* 33 (4), 380–397.

Public Health England, 2016. Health matters: Giving every child the best start in life. PHE: UK https://www.gov.uk/government/publications/health-matters-giving-every-child-the-best-start-in-life/health-matters-giving-every-child-the-best-start-in-life [Accessed 10/9/18].

6 Communicating through the environment

Catherine Gripton

OVERVIEW OF CHAPTER

Within an early years setting, the learning environment affords opportunities and possibilities for children to communicate with each other and with adults through their play, through representing their ideas (for example through painting or writing), and through their manipulation of resources as well as through their verbal and non-verbal interactions. These are explored in this chapter to contextualise communication within the environment before moving onto how the environment can be utilised to support communication where it is argued that open-ended resources and possibility-rich spaces are highly effective in enabling communication. The final section of this chapter points out that the environment is also a powerful communicator in itself. Essentially, the environment tells us what is important to the people in this place. As such, it provides key messages to children and their families about how they are perceived and valued within a setting. The environment provides subtle yet powerful messages about how children learn within it. It communicates which learning and development is most highly valued and what the adult and child roles are within this. This exploration of how the environment acts as a communicator is followed by a set of questions which offer opportunities to reflect upon the whole of this chapter and connect it to individual experiences and future practice.

Introduction

Early years practitioners recognise the vital importance of the learning environment for children's learning and development. It is the context through which communication is enabled or inhibited and practitioners spend enormous time and effort in creating learning environments which maximise the potential for learning.

The learning environment affords opportunities for children and adults to communicate, listen and think together in a wide range of ways. Resources, routines and practitioners enable the environment to act as a host for communication as well as providing the time, space, continuity and security which foster communication. Communication can therefore be perceived as acting as the intermediary that bridges the adult and child worlds.

The environment: a bridge between the adult and child

The learning environment can be considered as a conduit of learning for the child, connecting the child to possibilities for learning in a way which is meaningful and over which the child has ownership. The environment connects children with adults and other children within a shared community space and is vital in providing physical, emotional, and social spaces for learning and agency. Malaguzzi conceptualised the spatial environment as a "third educator" (Rinaldi 2006, p. 77) and as a flexible, responsive, and aesthetically beautiful place. This is an environment which a child contributes to creating and in which they can feel empowered, feel ownership, and feel safe. The environment, like a teacher, has an underpinning ethos and encapsulates beliefs about learning and values about education, children, and society. There is an argument, however, that perceiving the environment as an educator risks artificially separating environment from practitioner. We might instead consider the environment as an extension of the practitioner or group of practitioners. In this sense, creating the environment is an essential part of practitioner planning. Practitioners plan for learning through co-creating the environment with the children so that it contains endless possibilities for learning (Gripton 2017), limitless possible directions or pathways for learning. The environment is therefore like a bridge which connects children and practitioners. It is an intermediary between the adult world and the child's world, providing the context that translates meaning between the two.

The environment provides real and grounded contexts within which individual meanings are shared, negotiated and co-constructed. Within the environment, knowledge is socially constructed and communication made possible on all levels from more superficial cooperation to deeper shared thinking. The environment is a shared community space in which each individual is invested, what they feel to be "my space", and multiple perspectives are simultaneously represented. The mosaic approach (Clark and Moss 2011) acknowledges the importance of the environment and successfully utilises this understanding to support adults in gaining insight into children's perspectives. Research methods and assessment techniques such as child tours of environments, tracking observations, and children's photographs of their environment provide powerful documentation of children's perspectives within their worlds (see Chapter 3), particularly where children interpret these for themselves.

With the environment perceived to act as a bridge between adult and child, this connection is strengthened where children are perceived to have agency and a capacity to effect change and to co-construct the environment with practitioners. Vygotsky asserts that this requires us as practitioners to see children as more than social actors or social beings but as social agents and as active participants in society. The notion of children as social agents recognises them as more than attendees at a setting but as constructors of that setting. This aligns with an inclusive understanding that an early years setting IS the children, families, and practitioners that belong to it. It therefore changes and adapts with these people which requires an environment, as a bridge between adult and child, which is similarly adaptive.

Modes of communication and the multi-layered environment

Within the environment, we externalise our internal thinking through communicating. In doing so, we crystallise our thoughts, making them ready for sharing with others and capturing for ourselves. By committing to externalising our thinking through communication, we try out our internal understanding and test out ideas. This is far more sophisticated than a two-step process of thinking followed by communicating but is instead almost simultaneous. Thinking and communicating can be perceived as a self-perpetuating loop where we create, adapt and extend thinking whilst in the process of communicating it. We often, for instance, begin creating a sentence (whether verbal or written), or an image without knowing how we will complete it. The process of starting the sentence focusses our thinking and enables us to develop it "in the moment". The environment provides the context for this externalising of thinking and is therefore crucial in supporting children to develop thinking to communicate and to experience language to shape their thinking as well as to feel confident to share this thinking with others.

In creating the learning environment, we plan for possibilities in learning rather than outcomes of learning (Gripton 2017). To facilitate possibilities in learning, practitioners create environments that engage children and therefore stimulate communication where communication is not an end point or outcome but an integral part of the process of learning. Early years environments are where children create experiences worth communicating about and where communication authentically sustains, develops, and extends learning. These are multi-layered, incorporating the physical, emotional, and social learning environments.

In creating early years environments, we therefore need to consider enabling communication on physical, emotional, and social levels. This requires consideration of the physical layout, both indoors and outdoors, and of organisation of the setting, including systems, routines and staffing. These issues are explored later in this chapter.

Language is innately connected with thinking and shapes thought. Language development scaffolds understanding of the world by supporting children to make meaning and construct their individual sense of the world around them. It is therefore essential that the environment provides opportunities to listen to and observe others as they think and sense-make (both adults and children) and that thinking aloud, through articulation and many forms of representation, is encouraged and valued. Within an early years setting, the greater the possibilities for communication afforded by the learning environment, the greater the possibilities for thinking.

The emotional milieu in an early years environment is key in enabling children to take the risks involved in sharing their internal thoughts and understanding which can feel quite exposing to children and also to adults. As adults, there are times when we feel less confident to speak out or to show our written work. This is often where we feel less comfortable, where we worry that we might be judged, or when we are unsure whether others will agree or value our contributions. Reflecting upon how exposing it can feel as an adult can be helpful in considering this for children and enable us to think more deeply about how to create an effective learning environment for communication. Within a consistent and familiar environment where judgements are avoided and all contributions welcomed, communication is encouraged. Reducing both the size of the space in which we are communicating and the pressure upon "right answers" can also support communication. High stakes or performative communication needs to be kept to a minimum and where it is necessary, prepared for and anticipated. Crucially, where all forms of communication are valued and each individual's communication is deemed important, then a communication-rich environment is created.

The enormous range of modes of communication used by a child can be overlooked when considering communication from an educational perspective. There is a tendency in education systems to emphasise the modes of communication which appear easiest to measure. This is pointed out in Malaguzzi's popular "No Way, The Hundred is There" poem (translated by Gandini) where he points out:

The child has
a hundred languages
(and a hundred hundred hundred more)
but they steal ninety-nine.

The school and the culture
Separate the head from the body.
They tell the child to:
think without hands
to do without head
to listen and not to speak.

                                        (Edwards, Gandini, and Forman 2012, p. 3)

Within educational research there is a tendency to privilege written and spoken word above other forms of communication. Non-verbal communication data is significantly underrepresented in educational research despite much key meaning being communicated through modes of communication such as hand gestures (Denham and Onwuegbuzie 2013). As practitioners, we view communication in its widest sense and include gesture, facial expression, eye movement, body language, and other embodied communication as such. Within the environment, it is essential that we enable these forms of communication to be visible through ensuring that places to sit are positioned so that children and adults can see each other's faces and hands and that areas include sufficient space for whole body communication. On a practical level, this includes ensuring there is space for all children within a group to sit in a circle so that each individual can see every person in the group.

Pause, stillness (or lack of movement), and absence are often overlooked ways of communicating. Generally, these could indicate uncertainty or lack of confidence but could also communicate other things. Pausing within speech or movement might indicate a reformulation of thinking or consideration of others whereas inactivity could indicate opting out and not wanting to engage in an activity further or it could be that another priority is suddenly taking precedence, for example hunger. Children often move away from activities that they do not wish to participate in or avoid them altogether. It can be challenging to recognise these forms of communication as having equivalent importance to verbal expression of choices. Within a setting, ensuring that children have a genuine choice over where they play during child-initiated activity requires careful planning for provision to ensure that children are able to access all aspects of learning and development even if they do not access all physical spaces within the provision.

Whilst developing speech and language skills is an important aspect of our work as practitioners, we recognise that these support learning but should not inhibit or act as a barrier to it. Whilst language is representation in itself (representing through spoken or written words), representation within communication is broader than this. Speech and other forms of representation are often used fluidly together and these other forms are a significant mode of communication for all children. Representation within communication is intrinsically bound with context and therefore the environment is particularly essential within the development of communication with regards to representation. A child painting a picture, for example, is making deliberate marks to represent people, places, or feelings. A child pressing their finger to a wooden block, for example, might be using the block to represent a remote control within imaginative play. Children and adults regularly use objects, aesthetic materials (such as paint, collage, or pastel), utensils (for example brushes, pens, and pencils), malleable materials, and imaginative play to represent. It is therefore essential that children and adults have genuine access to these materials across the indoor and outdoor environment (that they believe they can and regularly do use these materials). Representation includes using words or numbers, creating images or diagrams, making structures or sculptures, choosing or creating models, using jotting or graphics, moving objects, and pretending. A representation holds meaning and significance to the creator but may require mediation, or at least time spent observing, for others to understand so adults need time in early years settings to observe, work in parallel, or engage in dialogue with children to facilitate this. This has clear implications for the organisation of the setting and roles of the practitioners within this.

Bruner (1966) categorised representations as enactive, iconic, or symbolic with all three important for children and adults. Within enactive representation, objects are associated with actions and meaning is made of objects. According to Bruner, with iconic representation images become "summarizers of action" (1966, p. 13) as images represent how a situation or action has been perceived by the individual. With symbolic representation, symbolic systems are used which are quite abstract but understood to relate to reality, for example, words or numerals. This can be a challenge for a child where different rules may apply for different systems. For example, nouns are used to name objects or ideas but number names represent a group of objects or the total counted so far. This means the same object can be given different number names, depending upon the order counted. Representations become more economical over time with a condensing down of meaning to the most efficient forms as the child develops, whilst still using all types of representation. Within the environment, we need to ensure that children have the opportunities to engage in representation using objects, images, and symbols regardless of developmental stage. There can be a tendency within education to remove or devalue objects or images as soon as a child shows a propensity for symbols whereas we all, including adults, need to represent with objects, images, and symbols and therefore require access to these within the environment. This is particularly important to encourage deeper and more challenging thinking as understanding can build over time through connecting several different representations of the same concept or idea.

Despite the importance of non-verbal communication, talk is not to be underestimated. It is important to perceive verbal and non-verbal communication as supportive of each other rather than competing or conflicting. Verbal communication is of particularly high importance in early years where it is often used as the mode of communication through which learning is negotiated and assessed, indeed it is emphasised within most early years curriculum documentation. Speaking and listening skills are therefore not just important as essential skills but are fundamental tools *for* learning. Speaking and listening are essential in all areas of learning, including mathematical, technological, scientific, social, artistic, physical, and musical learning, not merely literacy. Case Study 1 demonstrates an example of a child communicating their developing mathematical understanding in verbal, non-verbal, and recorded modes of communication.

CASE STUDY I

Maddie and Amy's Mathematical Graphics

Maddie and Amy were sharing pom-poms between them across a low table. Maddie pushed three pom-poms to Amy after taking three for herself. She slid three across the table without counting each one. Amy copied, giving Maddie three and then taking three for herself by sliding groups of three pom-poms under her hand. "Let's do it again", Maddie declared whilst sweeping all of them onto the floor. She grabbed a large sheet of paper from the rack behind her and placed it on the table then helped Amy put all of the pom-poms in a pile on top of it. They repeated their activity with Maddie sliding three to herself and then three to Amy. Amy did the same again, too. Maddie frowned and picked up a green marker pen. She drew a circle near to her and drew three circles inside. She then drew a circle near Amy and drew three dots. She held out the marker to Amy who tentatively took it and went over the three dots in her circle counting aloud "1, 2, 3 (more firmly for three)". Amy slowly drew a circle near to Maddie, looking to Maddie for affirmation. Amy drew three lines inside it and then moved to draw another circle nearer to herself followed by a line down the middle of the paper, back and forth to show which were her circles and which were Maddie's. Amy then drew four dots in her circle, perhaps intending to do three. The practitioner, who had been observing, asked Maddie how to write three to show she had been grouping in threes. Maddie made a "humph" sound and blew her fringe. She moved the marker pen forwards several times but did not use it on the paper. She paused then made an M on the paper. The practitioner gave a questioning look and Maddie stated "I'm three!" and offered the pen to Amy. Amy took it but passed it immediately to the practitioner, "I'm four!" she declared.

One important factor in enabling Maddie to communicate her mathematical thinking (Case Study 1) is the role of the adult. In the moment, the practitioner valued Maddie's mathematical graphics. The practitioner avoided judgement and instead tried to remain open, encouraging Maddie to continue to communicate and develop her thinking. This good practice "in the moment" was crucial to Maddie's success but perhaps of greater importance was the longer term work of the setting. The setting had endeavoured over time to provide an environment where jottings or graphics were valued as a mode of communication. One factor within this was the availability of large sheets of paper and large whiteboards so that children could engage in recording or developing thinking through jottings or graphics wherever they were working within the environment. Another essential factor was the practitioners regularly modelling jottings or graphics as a mode of communication. Through regularly seeing all practitioners record mathematical ideas using informal notation, Maddie saw this as something that good mathematicians (or clever people) do – a valuable way of communicating.

Children learn much about the relative importance of different modes of communication from adults. Where adults move within the environment communicates much to the child about what is valuable and valued within the setting. Children, therefore, need to see adults communicating in a full range of ways across the environment indoors and outdoors. Children need to see adults engaging in symbolic play, representing using objects, making informal jottings/graphics as well as using more abstract communication systems such as writing, speaking, and formal mathematical notation. Non-verbal communication can be particularly useful in sustaining conversations with children. A nod, quizzical look, pause, or open hand gesture can encourage a child to explain further, or in a new way, or to extend their idea. This practitioner communication should be authentic and purposeful. This means that practitioners ask questions for which they genuinely do not already know the answer, and communicate from inside children's play rather than outside of it. This can be asking a question as a character in role or to further an investigation rather than to tick off an assessment goal or curriculum target. Children's thinking can be closed down where they are distracted by an adult question which is outside of the task and thinking at hand. An example might be an adult asking how many wheels a car has when the child is exploring ramps to find the best one for launching a car across an imaginary river.

Possibilities for communication in the learning environment

Creating environments which maximise the possibilities for communication and are conducive to all modes of communication can be challenging. There are time, space, and financial restrictions which require creative practitioners and leaders to work within these limits in order to provide environments which maximise the potential for communication. Creating carefully structured "safe" social spaces is fundamental in achieving this. Many settings find it helpful to conceptualise this aim as to create "communication friendly spaces" (Jarman 2009) that encourage communication by providing smaller, cosier spaces which might perhaps feel more homely and will certainly make communication feel more comfortable. These social spaces should support communication by allowing children and adults to see each other's faces, enabling people to get close enough to hear each other and contain stimulating and cooperative resources to prompt communication and thinking. In practical terms, it can be helpful to have spaces in the environment which are appropriately sized for the people who use them and enable full body movement whilst having low ceilings and barriers or walls to define the space and reduce noise from elsewhere whilst also focussing attention inwards and upon each other.

Spaces within the environment should support holistic learning and development and not focus exclusively upon one area of the curriculum (Gripton 2017). It can be helpful to name spaces or areas by what they contain or provide rather than using names from the curriculum, to avoid confusion; a counting library or pattern area rather than a maths areas, for example. The term "meaningful spaces" might offer us support in reflecting upon provision for communication within the environment. Spaces should be meaningful to the children and connect to their previous experiences. They should feel in some sense familiar and be organised in such a way that they feel part of the child's world. A role play area themed as a place that is familiar to the child (a home rather than an office, for example) is a meaningful space within a learning environment. Similarly, a space where a child can lie on their stomach to play with small world toys might be more meaningful than a table and chair as the child has been lying on their stomach since they were a baby. Meaningful spaces feel natural to the child and are authentic. They acknowledge the real world of the child rather than an adult-invented notion of childhood that is brightly coloured, artificial, and plastic. Within meaningful spaces animal shaped furniture, vacuum cleaners that play music, and kitchen utensils with faces are replaced by simple, scaled down, or real furniture and resources.

Whilst meaningful spaces in the environment should feel safe, there needs to be an element of risk to facilitate new learning. Where learning is challenging, there is risk. It is risky to step outside of what you are sure of and attempt new things. The environment can include an element of physical risk such as within risky play. Risky play is often very exciting as it includes the potential for physical injury (Sandseter 2007). Within a learning environment, opportunities for physical risk-taking need to be included. This is not to say that an environment should be unsafe but that the opportunities to take physical risks should be apparent to children and to adults and appropriate to their physical capabilities. Essentially, this is the difference between one of the stepping stones being unsecure, which is unexpected for the child and clearly unsafe, and to them being quite far apart, yet secure and stable, so a child can choose to risk jumping from one to the other. The achievement of a challenge involving physical risk can be very gratifying to the child and encourage perseverance and resilience as they make many attempts over time. A child's interest in risky play can be communicated through their body language and facial expression, perhaps through putting their hand out to an adult or intensely looking at the location of risk. Practitioners need to be alert to the opportunities for risky play in the environment and also the ways that children might communicate that they are interested in taking a physical risk. Where the child communicates their interest in a physically risky activity through their body language, gesture, or facial expression, practitioners can communicate back to the child using the same modes of communication and join in with the risky play.

Where children find fascination within their environment and become highly involved with their play, they are almost compelled to communicate this in some way. Children might talk to themselves, record (perhaps photograph, draw, or write) or seek recognition by sharing with practitioners and other children. There are times when this communication is less deliberate and arises organically from the activity. In moments of absorption, children can lose inhibitions and naturally communicate this through noises (for example, a squeal of excitement) and through facial expressions. This is a key benefit of dizzy play where children are encouraged to momentarily lose and regain control. It is liberating and thrilling and in the moment of loss and regaining of control, more stubborn barriers to communication are temporarily lifted.

Providing the child with a reason or imperative to communicate, for example as in dizzy play, requires possibilities for communication within the environment. Resources are crucial to scaffolding and encouraging communication. If resources are deemed, like Frobel's gifts, to be an offer of the world to a child and a way to make their own sense of it, then we need to consider these resources with much care. We might look at each object within a learning environment and ask fundamental questions of it:

■ Does it deserve to be here?

■ Is it worthy of our children?

■ Is it sufficiently rich?

■ Does it offer the child opportunities to make their own meaning?

■ Does it provide opportunities for communication (representation, discussion, questions)?

Resources which offer only one option to the child, which can only ever be one thing, are limiting in terms of learning and communication. They offer only existing meanings from the adult world rather than affording the child the opportunity to make their own sense or their own meaning. Environments which include open-ended resources contain almost infinite possibilities to the child and encourage imagination, creativity, and ultimately communication as children communicate through the symbolic or representational meaning they have attributed to the resources. This encourages shared thinking as children and adults use shared meanings for resources; for example, together using the rectangular hole in the panel as an ice-cream van window.

CASE STUDY 2

The Talking Teddies

It is a few weeks into the beginning of the school year in the Reception class of 4–5 year olds and the team of practitioners meet to discuss planning for the following week. They are aware that many of the children are less engaged during carpet time sessions. Some children seem more focussed upon opening and closing the fastening on their shoes whilst others look out of the window or trace the carpet patterns with their fingers. The children seem engaged but generally in things other than the learning focus intended by the practitioners. The team discuss typical management strategies such as rewards, certain children sitting nearer to the practitioner or away from each other and more engaging session focusses. One practitioner comments that the children are engaged when it is their turn to speak, play the game, or hold the resources but that this engages only one or two children at a time. Another explains that "talk partners" works well with older children but requires speaking and listening skills that the children are currently developing and not yet consistently all able to use. There is a moment's pause before she poses the question, "do the talk partners need to be people?" The team excitedly discuss possibilities before deciding upon "talking teddies". A bag of cuddly toys are recycled from the Christmas fayre leftovers and placed in baskets around the carpet area. Next day, the children are asked to choose a talking teddy and give it a name. Each carpet time, the children get their talking teddy from the basket and explain to the teddy what is happening in the session. They tell their teddy their individual responses to questions posed by the practitioners, show them the numbers of fingers when counting, explain why an answer is right or wrong, tell the teddy their opinion or prediction, and report back their child-initiated learning to the teddy at the end of a session. The talking teddies improved engagement and communication as well as supporting thinking through enabling communication. They also had unintended outcomes such as providing a companion for when children felt anxious or upset and a reading buddy to share books with.

A rich environment contains open-ended resources and meaningful spaces which encourage communication but might also facilitate it through providing someone to communicate with. Whilst social spaces within a setting provide opportunities for and encourage social interaction, resources can provide others with whom they can communicate, within and beyond the setting. Children can communicate with members of the local community, toys, animals, and book characters as well as their own families. Case Study 2 provides an example of how one setting provided each child with an audience for their communication and therefore increased communication within their setting.

Opportunities to communicate to an audience beyond the setting include online message board posts, models, pictures, greetings cards, letters, instructions, notices, and telephone calls, usually imaginary. Within the environment, providing resources such as a post box, old mobile telephones, a display board for messages, a secure online message board, envelopes and sticky notes can provide the children with a reminder of the wider potential audiences for their communication. Communication to a wider audience can include video and voice communication by using technology such as talking tins, talking pens, and tablets or cameras with video capabilities. These can involve consideration of the ethical and security issues of such communication as explained by Cazaly in her chapter.

The environment as communicator

High quality, open-ended resources and meaningful spaces communicate much to the child and their family about them being valued by the setting. Subtle yet powerful values and perceptions of people are communicated through representation of diversity within displays, documentation, and resources (see Peart's chapter for an exploration of this in regard to race and culture). How families are represented is particularly important, ensuring that the full range of family groupings are represented including families with same-sex parents, single parents, multiple birth children, grandparents, and parents/children with disabilities. On a practical level, this includes forms that ask for "name(s) of parent(s)" rather than names of mother and father as well as representative small world toys and picture books.

Much is communicated through the environment to children and families about the nature of learning, the values of the setting, and the expectations of the children. Routines and organisation or presentation of resources communicate what is expected of the child including whether they are expected to be independent, autonomous, and make decisions. The placement of furniture and resources communicates what is most important in a setting. A large adult chair as a central focus or area labelled as belonging to an adult, such as Mrs Smith's carpet area, communicates the central importance and ownership of that area by the adult. Books and displays can communicate the importance of outdoor learning, educational visits, or the local community by making these prominent features of a setting. Similarly, ensuring all children have their photographs or creative endeavours on display can communicate an inclusive ethos. Some settings choose to give each child their own small display space which they curate and change for themselves which communicates a child-led philosophy.

Children see what is valued and valuable by where the adults spend most time in the environment and how they use it. This is evident in Case Study 1 where Maddie created her own mathematical graphics as part of the everyday communication of her mathematical thinking. She had observed adults, who were important to her, regularly interacting with the environment and communicating in this way. The adult's regular interaction with and within the environment communicates to the child both what we do here and what is important in this place.

The environment, as a physical shared space, can be used to connect individuals in many ways. Using the metaphor of the environment as a bridge, examples were considered earlier in this chapter of the environment connecting the adult and child. Similarly, the environment can connect practitioners. The environment of an early years setting can be used effectively as the basis for professional development where the practitioner team can engage in a more structured audit of the physical environment or less structured walk around the environment to view it through the eyes of a child. It can support reflection through stepping back and looking with fresh eyes.

A team of practitioners might individually or in pairs take a different perspective and explore the environment from that perspective. Perspectives might include: new parent, parent and child for whom English is an additional language, child who feels anxious, grandparent, community member, practitioner from another setting, practitioner working with older children, older sibling, child with a physical disability, health practitioner, younger and older child, child from an under-represented ethnic minority, same-sex parents, a setting leader, play worker, and a child who feels energetic. In some settings, leaders occasionally navigate their way around a setting on their knees to see what it looks like from the height of a child and it provides significant insight into what is accessible and easily viewed. At a basic level, this provides information about what is within children's reach and whether the hastily stored resources pushed under a table are really as hidden as one might think they are when viewed from an adult height.

The questions that follow could be used within staff training or professional development as a prompt for shared team reflection. They might open up professional dialogue and support a review or refocus upon setting ethos and vision using the physical environment as a way of depersonalising and stepping back from the practice of individuals. It is intended that some of these questions may be pondered over for several days or longer rather than eliciting an immediate response and could be posed as a reflective question of the week or term as well as one-off events.

PROVOCATIONS

- What is your ideal learning environment? What does it look/feel/sound like? To the child? To the adult? To the parent?

- How could you make an area of the learning environment more meaningful to the children, more inviting as a social space or more valuing of all modes of communication?

- Think about an early years environment that is very familiar to you. In the presentation of resources, decoration of the walls/displays, labelling of the environment, organisation of the session/day, and timetabling of adults, what messages are communicated to children and parents?

- Upon entering an early years setting, what is most prominent and what is less immediate? What might this suggest about the values of the setting? What might this say to a child or parent about what is valued and important?

References

Bruner, J.S., 1966. *Toward a Theory of Instruction*. London: Belknap Press.

Clark, A., and Moss, P., 2011. *Listening to Young Children: The Mosaic Approach*. London: NCB.

Denham, M.A., and Onwuegbuzie, A.J., 2013. Beyond Words: Using Nonverbal Communication Data in Research to Enhance Thick Description and Interpretation. *International Journal of Qualitative Methods*, 12 (1), 670–696.

Edwards, C.P., Gandini, L., and Forman, G.E., eds., 2012. *The Hundred Languages of Children: The Reggio Emilia Experience in Transformation*. 3rd ed. Oxford: Praeger.

Gripton, C., 2017. Planning for Endless Possibilities. In: A. Woods, ed., *Child-initiated Play and Learning: Planning for Possibilities in the Early Years*. 2nd ed. London: David Fulton, pp. 8–22.

Jarman, E., 2009. *The Communication Friendly Spaces Approach: Improving Speaking, Listening, Emotional Well-being and General Engagement*. Bethersden: Elizabeth Jarman Limited.

Rinaldi, C., 2006. *In Dialogue with Reggio Emilia: Listening, Researching, and Learning*. London: Routledge.

Sandseter, E.B.H., 2007. Categorising Risky Play: How Can we Identify Risk-taking in Children's Play? *European Early Childhood Education Research Journal*, 15 (2), 237–252.

7 A child's image and their toys

Sheine Peart

OVERVIEW OF CHAPTER

This chapter explores how children's images are reflected in toys and dolls. It reviews the impact of this symbolic representation and the overt and hidden messages which can be communicated through imagery. It considers the legal requirement to promote equality of opportunity in society and the workplace and makes specific links of the importance of this legislation for early years educators. It provides a historical context for how some Black communities came to make the UK their home and the way the growing population of Black and minority ethnic children in education settings has heightened the need for a strategic, structural response to support inclusion of all cultures. It considers the impact of race and identity construction and what this can mean for children from minority ethnic groups and the implications for early years practitioners. It assesses the impact of misrepresentation on identity, how omission subliminally communicates who belongs within a community, and the importance of accurate representation. The chapter concludes by providing some guidance of importance of culturally representative toys and resources.

Introduction

Children interact with and react to their environments on a constant basis and environments convey powerful messages about the world children occupy. Children are immersed in these environments which communicate a multitude of spoken and unspoken messages about a child's location within and its relationship to the wider world. Children absorb this information verbally, visually and emotionally and use this information to enable them to develop schemata and conceptual frameworks of the world, which in turn help them to understand their immediate and wider environments. Within this world one of the principal communication vehicles are the toys and games children play with. Toys and games matter because they are one of the tools children use to help them understand the world. Toys can communicate messages of hope and possibility, they can inspire and enthuse children, providing ideas to fire young imaginations. Children, use toys to help them reconstruct their world and to develop their appreciation of how that world operates. Consequently, toys and the environment also have the capacity to communicate racially constructed views of the world, an idea supported by Pitcher, who comments

> It's interesting to think about the ways in which ideas about race are produced and reproduced in children's media, games and toys. Racial enculturation, the practice of learning about race, is just as much part of growing up as any other significant element of human culture.
>
> (Pitcher 2014, p. 89)

The potential problem here is if children are given flawed or incorrect information they may develop false, inappropriate, or possibly even harmful views and attitudes potentially configuring some groups of people as crude, negative racialised stereotypes, or persons of no significance. Alternatively, if children never see themselves represented in toys, they may develop the view that they do not belong in certain environments. Helpfully, in the UK there is legislative and statutory guidance which works to promote positive attitudes towards race and to counter the potential damage negative or inaccurate messages can produce. The 2010 Equality Act places a legal requirement on all organisations (public, private, and community) to take action to

> Advance equality of opportunity between people who share a [protected] characteristic and those who don't;
>
> Foster good relations between people who share a [protected] characteristic and those who don't.
>
> (Equality and Human Rights Commission 2018)

Under the Equality Act race is specifically identified as a protected characteristic and all providers must work to engender and encourage positive relationships between different groups and to openly convey messages to children of the value of all communities.

The impact of the environment on children's development is examined in this chapter through a critical race theory lens. The chapter considers how the environment communicates openly and subtly with children in early years' settings and how the presence or absence of globally representational resources and imagery may contribute to a child's well-being and understanding of self. The chapter develops the theme of how practitioners need to ensure they are using different resources which accurately reflect wider society, reinforcing the concept of a culturally diverse global community in which all children are valued, valuable, and belong. The chapter provides a historical context for the presence of some Black populations in the UK and considers contemporary changes in national demographics. It tasks practitioners and educationalists to examine their own settings to discover how these environments challenge negative, stereotypical presentations and support the notion of a culturally diverse inclusive society based on sound ethics and values.

Choosing resources for children

Consider the representations of people in your setting. Think about the dolls, small world play figures, images on puzzles, and in books

- What are your initial instinctive responses to each image?

- In what circumstances would/could you use these images?

- What messages do you feel these representations communicate to children?

- How do you think the children in your settings would react/interact with these resources?

Changing demographics in the UK

Britain has a long history of cultural and racial diversity. There have been Black people in Britain for almost 2,000 years and Britain was once ruled by a Black emperor, Septimius Severus, a North African, from AD 193–211. As a result of the Roman Empire Black people came to the UK as enlisted soldiers and traders; some of whom stayed and some formed partnerships with the indigenous population securing a continued Black presence. During the Transatlantic Slave Trade, unknown numbers of Black people were brought to England in captivity to work. However, in 1772 in a landmark legal judgement Lord Chief Justice Mansfield ruled slavery was "so odious that nothing could be suffered to support it" (National Archives 1772) and the 14,000 slaves then living in Britain were immediately pronounced freed. Later in 1948 members of the Caribbean were invited to work in Britain by the government to help with post-war structural and economic reconstruction. In 1972 when Idi Amin ordered the compulsory expulsion of Ugandan Asians, over 27,000 migrated and made their home in the UK. Once again, some of these migrants formed partnerships with the home population which has contributed to a growing number of Black children in the UK. Currently "the ethnic minority population in the UK is increasing" (National Audit Office 2008, p. 4) and Britain's mixed race population is expected to be the largest minority ethnic group in the UK by 2020. As a direct consequence of national demographic changes the number of children from minority ethnic groups in early years and school settings is also increasing.

The changing demographic landscape of Britain presents opportunities, questions, and for some early years settings, challenges to practices and processes. As the population changes and evolves, families and communities require settings to change to meet their needs. The legislative framework of the 2010 Equality Act, the requirements of the Statutory Framework for the Early Years Foundation Stage (EYFS) (Department for Education 2017) and a declared government ambition to build stronger, more cohesive communities, make it imperative for all early years settings to embed equality in all aspects of their work and provision. Within the context of a long standing and growing Black population in Britain, the need for inclusion of multiple, diverse cultures is a moral and educational necessity for all educators.

The Importance of identity

All children need to develop an accurate sense of self. They need to understand who they are and how they relate with and to others in close and wider circles. Working out a personal identity is a "central absorbing task for 3-, 4- and 5-year olds" (Derman-Sparks and the A.B.C Task Force 2001, p. 31). Children are in the process of working out the people they will eventually become; a process which starts at birth and is developed through immersion, education, and experience. Identity is a complex bricolage of multiple features. Some features are fixed and immutable (even if a child expresses a preference to be with a pet dog and proclaims a wish to be a dog, it is not possible to change species), while other features will almost certainly change with the passage of time (it is unlikely all food tastes from childhood will remain as the child grows and matures). However, each of these different facets is an important signifier of personal and group identity. Offering staple carbohydrates such as rice or yam as well as potatoes and bread on a nursery menu indicates a child's diet is not strange or exotic, but is one of many different common foods. Children rapidly become aware of the ways they are similar to and different from others in terms of physical differences such as skin colour or facial features and more nuanced socially constructed features including diet and musical tastes and are sophisticated enough to observe some characteristics such as gender, economic status, and race have the capacity to confer power and privilege to certain groups or individuals while other features appear to produce disadvantage.

While "race has been discredited as a meaningful biological category" (Anderson 2010, p. 32) it remains a powerful social construct which informs and shapes our personal and public identity. Race is often understood as a set of shared characteristics including skin colour and other physical features which link individuals together and is frequently conflated with culture, geography, religious affiliation, and common historical experiences. Unhelpful or inaccurate stereotypes about different racial groups may curtail or limit children's opportunities. Race can assume further potency through preconceptions which influence individuals' beliefs and perceptions of some groups. Although race is a contestable concept its progeny, racism, exerts significant influence on the life chances of children and adults alike. For example, a practitioner who believes African and Caribbean children are only good at sports may focus on primarily developing a child's physical abilities and may give less attention to other endeavours such as literacy or numeracy.

CASE STUDY

Making Music

Tony, a White English male, worked in a pre-school setting attached to his local primary school. Tony had a firm belief in representing different cultures in his work and believed in involving the local community wherever and whenever possible. Having some Black musician friends, Tony decided to invite in his colleagues to provide a session on African drumming and dance to which he also invited the children's parents and carers. The children seemed to enjoy the session and were fully engaged. However, at the end of the session, one parent remarked to another on leaving that she could "not see the point in all this politically correct stuff" and wondered why "traditional English nursery rhymes had gone out of fashion".

"All children's racial identities are important" (Lane 2008, p. 135) as race is intimately linked to our personal construction of individual identity which in turn informs what we believe about ourselves, what we consider we are capable of achieving and areas and opportunities we believe are prohibited. It is through the capacity to participate that we develop a sense of community which strengthens our identity. Our successes produce a sense of achievement which nurtures our self-esteem and conception of our capabilities, which, in a self-fulfilling feedback loop, further feeds our "construction of personal identity - of how we define and understand ourselves as individuals" (James and James 2012, p. 49). Identity is important to children because it supports a sense of belonging and through affirming children's sense of worth, provides a psychological and cultural base from which a child may explore and experiment.

Children's identities are fuelled and sustained by the environments in which they are located and operate within and by the artefacts found in those settings. Early years providers are in a key position to influence and promote positive messages about a child's identity and culture. When early year's settings display positive imagery of other cultures and nations, the setting is implicitly stating different cultures are welcomed and valued enabling children to develop a secure sense of self and promoting confidence. When children can see the environment values their culture and by implication them, the child is "more likely to be motivated to learn from what the setting has to offer" (Lane 2008, p. 135). However, it is important settings remain mindful of variation within communities and families and are not tempted to consider all children from certain communities or all family members are the same. While it is essential to have an understanding of multiple cultures, settings must recognise "individual differences" (Mercer 2018, p. 27) and value the uniqueness of each child.

Children need to feel positive about themselves and know they are wanted and belong. It is only once a Black child has "achieved an identity ... [they can] ... successfully navigate the demands of different social contexts" (Brittain 2012, p. 173). All children are in need of access to culturally diverse resources to support the development of a positive self-identity and to enable them to develop an accurate understanding of their immediate and other communities. Cultural diversity should not be considered a competition between different groups and practitioners should avoid giving the impression of a hierarchy of status among different cultures or communities. Practitioners need to include broad representation of different cultures at all stages in their work from planning to delivery to evaluation and need to create opportunities to engage with wider communities. Practitioners need to include material and experiences which draw on and utilise the wealth of knowledge and experience across cultural groups, drawing on resources that may already exist in the local community. At times this may mean breaking with current conventions and changing practice which may produce new challenges. If change is met with resistance either within or outside the setting, practitioners need to remember the goals of early year's education and try to work with detractors to educate them in the benefits of cultural inclusion.

Goals of the EYFS

The inclusive approach promoted by the 2010 Equality Act is further supported by

> The EYFS statutory framework [which] sets the standards that all early years providers must meet to ensure that children learn and develop well ... [and] provide the right foundation for good future progress through school and life.
> (Standards and Testing Agency 2017, p. 8)

The EYFS framework confirms the principle that "every child deserves the best possible start in life and the support that enables them to fulfil their potential" (Department for Education 2017, p. 5). The framework further asserts a "secure safe and happy childhood is important in its own right" (ibid.). The framework establishes that settings must provide "equality of opportunity and anti-discriminatory practice, ensuring that every child is included and supported" (ibid.). The early years curriculum adopts a child centred approach which recognises the distinctiveness of each child and is underpinned by an implicit expectation that children should be supported to develop a positive self-image so they can form productive relationships with others in differing settings including school and their community.

The EYFS strives to encourage all children to develop a positive self-image and to be respectful of other cultures (Early Education 2012). The EYFS recognises the importance of promoting diversity through play and the importance of reflecting different cultures in resources including toys, games, and books to help children understand their environment and the wider world.

Within the EYFS particular emphasis is placed upon children developing an informed understanding of the wider world in which all communities are valued and recognises that children learn through play and using their senses. Because children are instinctively inquisitive and curious, practitioners need to provide children with real or realistic resources to help them learn. Play and learning opportunities need to include diverse representation of cultures, so that cultural representation is not an isolated tokenistic event but becomes an integral part of routine practice and is woven into the fabric of working life.

Communicating through resources: the impact of misrepresentation on identity

It is important to remember that in order to effectively support children, early years practitioners need to have a keen awareness of what leads to healthy development (Brittain 2012). From the 1950s to the 1970s the representation of Black people in toys and games bordered on the grotesque. Black female dolls were commonly portrayed as surprised naked picaninnies or household slaves such as "mammy dolls". Black male dolls were represented as equally inaccurate golliwogs with ill-formed grossly exaggerated lips and eyes. In contrast to White dolls and toys, Black dolls were portrayed as unattractive and were shown as figures to be ridiculed or feared. Golliwogs also provided the truncated dual racist slurs for all people of African and Caribbean heritage of golly and wog. While most toys are mass produced and lack the individuality seen in human populations, golliwogs and mammy dolls also had the impact of reinforcing ideas of ugliness and supporting the idea of "out group homogeneity" (Anderson 2010, p. 28) where the individuality of each person is ignored. Although such toys would now not be considered suitable for use in early years settings they have bequeathed a racist language which is still in use today. An inherent problem of these short syllable words is they are easy to pronounce and simple to learn for even very young children and perversely provide a "child-friendly" accessible racist vocabulary. The continuing legacy of these toys was the normalisation of racist language for all children and the continued damaging othering of Black children.

The crude iconography and racist imagery of these dolls and toys was further underlined by popular media culture of the time which provided 'The Black and White Minstrels' television show and gollies were used as a marketing image for jams and preserves. While a warped interpretation of the presence of golly and picaninny toys could be suggested to represent ethnic diversity and inclusion, this imagery was inaccurate, negative, and for some children frightening. These toys did not present an affirmative representation of Black people or provide an image many Black children would wish to associate with, and most children would not express an ambition to be a house slave.

The depiction was not warm or friendly but startling and unsettling and served to portray Black people as gruesome, monstrous outsiders who could only be included as part of mainstream society in a subservient capacity. The persistent "misrepresentation of Black culture ... continued reinforcement of negative stereotypes ... may contribute to feelings of anger" (Brittain 2012) in Black children and hinder the development of a positive identity. To include golliwogs or mammy dolls in children's play gives tacit approval to racist imagery and by implication racism through normalising racist attitudes and positioning Black people as outsiders or characters of lesser worth.

One of the impacts of misrepresentation and its embedded racism was starkly demonstrated by experimental psychologists Clark and Clark in the 1950s. Extending their earlier work on race consciousness in children, Clark and Clark conducted a series of powerful studies on doll preference with groups of Black and White children. Given a choice many children preferred dolls with "a White skin color and rejected a brown skin color" (Clark and Clark 1950, p. 341) and when children were offered either a White skinned or Black skinned doll to play with there was a "clear-cut rejection of brown as a skin color (sic) preference" (ibid., p. 349). Further, this rejection was "most marked in dark [skinned] children" (ibid.). At the time Clark and Clark attributed this rejection among Black children as a recognition that "to be colored (sic) in American society is a mark of inferior status" (ibid., p. 350). As a result children actively chose the White skinned doll because they recognised the enhanced status of White people in society, introducing issues of "inadequacy and inferiority" (ibid.) and a "fundamental conflict at the very structure of the ego foundation" (ibid.) for the Black children in the study.

In a similar study in 2015 to determine ethnic preference by children, Willis and Lander carried out a picture investigation with children from different ethnic groups in the UK. Using images of children of different ethnicities they found "all pupils … held negative stereotypes of ethnic minority people" (Willis and Lander 2015, p. 40) considering Black people to be "unhappy, poor and naughty" (ibid., p. 39) or ascribing other negative characteristics to Black people such as dirty, unclean, or untruthful.

Representation matters as both Clark and Clark and Willis and Lander's work demonstrates, an environment populated by negative imagery damages Black children's ability to work out their role in society and may suggest to other children that Black children are less important. Clark and Clark claimed "negative images of Black people are bound to do damage to children trying to understand their place in society" (1950, p. 341). Rather than being able to filter and reject these messages, Swanson et al. claim some children "internalise biases" (2009, p. 274), accept racist messages, and start to think of themselves as being worthless "unless there is active and consistent intervention to minimize the influence" (ibid.). Such intervention must be taken up by all leaders, managers, and all staff in early years settings. Effective intervention can only be achieved through an active process of racial socialization which values and includes all. Toys and dolls are one way to show this active positive inclusion. In themselves representative dolls cannot prevent racism but they are a resource to help children value themselves more and "develop positive self-images" (ibid., p. 272) and to demonstrate to other children that all communities are welcomed in the setting.

CASE STUDY

Engaging Families

Clare, an EYFS practitioner, thought it would be a good idea to try and reach out more to her local community. As part of a timeline project to help children learn more about the past, Clare asked the children to bring in books, toys, and games from older family relatives. Amy brought in a copy of "Little Black Sambo" and informed Clare it was her grandmother's "favourite book". Clare was pleased with the local community's engagement and wanted to recognise Amy's contribution, however, she was uncertain what to do with the book Amy had given her.

The significance of omission for Black children

Further difficulties in representation are created when settings choose to adopt a colour-blind approach and do not recognise the unique features of an individual's identity. In practice this often means adopting the mores and norms of the dominant culture and omitting any positive representation of Black people. When imagery of Black "children [is] absent" (Roethler 1998, p. 97) it presents a skewed picture of contemporary society and tacitly implies Black people have no "place in this society" (ibid.). Omission effectively configures society as a "no-Black" zone and positions "the Black child an interloper" (ibid., p. 98). This is detrimental to the Black child because it conveys the message Black children do not belong and are not wanted which, in turn, "undermines self-perception" (ibid. p. 98). It is these "subtle, subconscious, subliminal ways [which] influence the way children perceive the world in which they live and the way they act and react in it" (ibid.). In this way harm is caused to the Black child because the picture presented to the child is a world in which they have no rightful place. As a result, the child is denied the tools needed to enable them to create personalised schemata in which they belong. The child cannot clearly identify their role and is unable to understand what sorts of roles (parent, plumber, or politician) they might aspire to. Omission makes the Black child a stranger, an outsider, part of the "them" population, never part of the mainstream "us".

Black children need to be given the means and guidance which helps them "to envision a future for themselves, and tools which they will use as they grow to deal with situations which arise in their lives" (ibid., p. 100). Adults and other significant others need to "use scaffolding techniques to foster cultural pride in young children" (Swanson et al. 2009, p. 271). Culturally sensitive inclusive toys are part of this process. Lego figures which represent Katherine Johnson, a Black female mathematician whose work on orbital mechanics was pivotal in the success of the 1960s American space programme and Mae Jemison, the first Black woman astronaut, are an important part of indicating to Black children they are capable of the highest level of achievement and are significant members of society with valuable contributions to make. Toys like this help to reinforce the heterogeneity and talents within the Black community and break the cycle of low expectations and patronising attitudes. Toys help children imagine possibilities and create new and different realities.

The importance of accurate and positive representation

Accurate representation of Black people in toys is important for Black children because it helps them develop a positive self-identity and supports managing and coping skills which will be needed in different situations in life. White children and other ethnic groups need to see positive representation of Black people to help them avoid forming stereotypical damaging views of Black people. In the 1950s Clark and Clark identified the need to relieve Black children of "the tremendous burden of feelings of inadequacy and inferiority" (1950, p. 350) created through oppression, omission, and misrepresentation. Contemporary society needs and demands toys that help children accommodate and value difference, toys which help children mature and confidently face the challenges they may experience as they grow older. Dolls should not be caricatures and "not all Blacks look alike" (Roethler 1998, p. 101). Because play is "an integral part of socialization of children" (ibid., p. 103) children need toys, games, and dolls which accurately reflect society and "stimulate thought, esteem, and creativity [to] help them to develop into competent, caring, responsible adults" (ibid.). It is important for educational settings to incorporate "culturally relevant materials and activities into children's experience" (Swanson et al. 2009, p. 274) so children may develop a candid understanding of the world and the skills needed to benefit from life's opportunities and to manage life's problems. When Black children are equipped with tools and strategies they need, they are more confident, more resilient and better able to "negotiate [the] challenges of positive Black identity within a social context" (ibid.).

In 2009 ABC news repeated the Clark and Clark experiments during the Obama administration with 19 Black children. In contrast to the initial experiment where Black children rejected the Black doll, this time the researchers found "88 per cent of the children happily identified with a dark-skinned doll" and many children "thought they too could be president one day" (Guy 2017). Although this was an important finding, a measure of caution is necessary because of the small sample size. While such a positive reaction is unlikely to be solely attributable to Obama's presidency (other positive affirmative work was probably undertaken by families, friends, and educators) seeing a Black president, having a strong, positive role model to aspire to and seeing such an office was possible shifted mind sets. Rather than rejecting their ethnicity most Black children now embraced their identity and cultural heritage, welcoming the opportunity to play with Black dolls which further helped to support the child's sense of self. Representation at all levels, from toys to public office, matters because it signifies inclusion. Dolls matter because children need to see and recognise themselves in the world and need the help of racially representative toys to help them build a world in which they have a meaningful role. Without such support children may internalise extant views and attitudes "resulting in a poor self-concept and self-hatred" (Swanson et al. 2009, p. 270). Representation subliminally suggests what a child can achieve, where they are included as a matter of course and a matter of right; a place where they do not have to fight, beg, or plead to be given an opportunity. Representation releases possibility and provides them with the support needed to release potential.

CASE STUDY

It's Only a Game

Pam, a nursery manager, has asked her team to observe children's reactions to some new resources she had purchased. Ian, a member of staff reported that two young boys in his care, Peter and Sam, were unhappy about the football figures that had been bought because the toys did not look like the people in the boys' favourite team, Chelsea. When Ian talked with the children about this they told Ian the players they liked best were N'Golo Kanté and Antonio Rüdiger two Black players in the Chelsea team. Sam also mentioned his Dad had said all the best football players were Black, like him. When Ian asked the boys their thoughts on Ross Barkley and Danny Drinkwater, two White English players on the Chelsea squad, the boys replied they were ok but not as good as the Black players.

Availability of toys and resources

To help develop their understanding of different cultures, children need access to a range of culturally representative resources. However, locating such resources can be challenging. While most toy stores and supermarkets hold a wide stock of White dolls, fewer outlets have Black dolls. According to a 2017 survey for the BBC, when families tried to purchase Black or African Caribbean toys for their children from high street stores, they found "their retail options were significantly reduced" (Smith and Lewis 2017) and toy manufacturers claim there is insufficient demand to warrant producing such toys. Indeed, Zapf Creation decided to cease production of a Black baby doll in 2014. While Mattel produce a number of Barbie dolls which appear to be from different ethnic groups, these dolls have been heavily criticised as neither the features nor the hair are accurately representative of Black African and Caribbean people.

Noticing the level of under and misrepresentation in the market, other manufacturers have responded to this issue and produced more culturally accurate toys. These toys include Rooti dolls which are more anatomically accurate and speak African languages to help children develop a better understanding of African culture. However, many of these toys are not readily available in high street shops and families wishing to purchase Black dolls either need to find these toys on the internet or request they are collected by friends and family visiting other countries. Further, in comparison to White dolls some of these toys are prohibitively expensive for many families.

If Black and White families find it difficult or too expensive to purchase Black dolls, children may not have the opportunity to play with Black dolls. This raises important leadership issues for early years providers in terms of the resources purchased for the setting and questions how to spend the setting's budget. Aubrey (2011) states early years leaders need to be able to clearly explain a vision for their setting and need to remain responsive to change. If children are to develop an accurate, respectful understanding of different cultures, they need to be appropriately supported. Education has long accepted the responsibility of providing children with opportunities the home background cannot. Within the context of the EYFS, settings need to ensure they have appropriate resources to enable all children to develop an accurate cultural awareness of differing populations. If the implication here is to purchase certain kinds of resources, the setting needs to exercise strong moral leadership and meet this obligation.

CASE STUDY

Making the Right Choice?

After much deliberation Eleanor (who is mixed race, Black African-Caribbean and White English) and her partner Barnabe (who is Black French African-Caribbean) moved from London to a smaller town in the Midlands when a job opportunity arose. The family were pleased to move, reasoning their two children, Thierry, two, and David, three, would be able to play outside more as they grew older, something both parents wanted and was not easily achievable in London. As both Eleanor and Barnabe mostly worked from home this seemed a pragmatic choice as it would give their children more freedom.

To help prepare Thierry and David for school their parents wanted the children to attend pre-school so their sons could become used to socialising with other children. Once they had re-located Eleanor and Barnabe researched pre-school provision in their area. They identified three settings they thought might be suitable for their two children. However, when they visited each setting Eleanor and Barnabe were surprised at how few resources the settings had which positively reflected their children's backgrounds. When the couple enquired what the settings' policies were on cultural diversity they were disappointed to be told "Not many Black children live around here. We haven't seen the need to do anything special". As Eleanor and Barnabe are new to the area they do not yet have a network of family and friends who might be able to offer support with looking after the two boys and while both parents could care for the children as they work from home the couple strongly feel culturally appropriate childcare which recognises different heritages should be readily available.

Chapter summary

In the early stages of development children are susceptible to messages communicated in many different ways. They notice who is in their world and who is influential. They can see and hear differences between people. Although some of these differences are fixed physical features, children may learn other behaviours from adults and their surroundings regarding belonging and respect. The legislative framework in the UK makes it a legal obligation for all early year practitioners to encourage integration and to provide positive representation of all cultures. If children are not provided with appropriate resources and support, they may develop false ideas and negative attitudes towards some groups. Early years practitioners need to be pro-active and work to ensure that children are not given inaccurate information and have the skills and attitudes needed in today's global community. The case studies throughout this chapter have demonstrated the significance of resources on a child's development. Early years leaders, managers, and practitioners need to be mindful of the environment they are creating for children and show leadership at all stages of planning and delivery to promote positive representation of diverse groups and provide children with embedded opportunities to explore, ask questions, and learn about different cultures.

PROVOCATIONS

■ Reflecting on the information you have read in this chapter, conduct a resource evaluation of the toys and play equipment available in your setting. What global communities are included and how are they represented?

■ What do your current resources communicate to children and their families about cultural inclusion?

■ What actions, if any, are needed to ensure your workplace accurately and fairly represents different ethnic groups?

■ Who is responsible for purchasing toys and resources for the setting?

References

Anderson, K.J., 2010. *Benign Bigotry: The Psychology of Subtle Prejudice*. Cambridge: Cambridge University Press.
Aubrey, C., 2011. *Leading and Managing in the Early Years*. London: Sage.

Brittain, A.S., 2012. Understanding African American Adolescents' Identity Development: A Relational Developmental Systems Perspective. *The Journal of Black Psychology*, 38 (2), 172–200.

Clark, K.B. and Clark, M.P., 1950. Emotional Factors in Racial Identification and Preference in Negro Children. *The Journal of Negro Education*, 19 (3), 431–350.

Department for Education, 2017 *Statutory Framework for the Early Years Foundation Stage*, Department for Education. Available at: https://assets.publishing.service.gov.uk/government/uploads/system/uploads/attachment_data/file/596629/EYFS_STATUTORY_FRAMEWORK_2017.pdf [Accessed 02.06.2018].

Derman-Sparks and the A.B.C. Task Force, 2001. *Anti-Bias Curriculum, Tools for Empowering Young Children*. Washington D.C.: National Association for the Education of Young Children, United States of America.

Early Education, 2012. *Development Matters in the Early Years Foundation Stage (EYFS)*. London: British Association for Early Childhood Education.

Equality and Human Rights Commission. *The Public Sector Equality Duty* Available at: https://www.equalityhumanrights.com/en/corporate-reporting/equality-and-diversity/public-sector-equality-duty [Accessed 21.09.2018].

Guy, J., 2017. *The Role and Lasting Effects of Dolls in the African American Community*. Available at: https://www.linkedin.com/pulse/role-lasting-effects-dolls-african-american-community-jasmine-guy/ [Accessed 03.03.2018].

James, A. and James, A., 2012. *Key Concepts in Childhood Studies*. London: Sage.

Lane, J., 2008. *Young Children and Racial Justice: Taking Action for Racial Equality in the Early Years – Understanding the Past, Thinking about the Present, Planning for the Future*. London: National Children's Bureau.

Mercer, J., 2018. *Child Development Concepts and Theories*. London: Sage.

National Archives, 1772. *Somerset Case*. Available at: http://www.nationalarchives.gov.uk/pathways/Blackhistory/rights/docs/state_trials.htm [Accessed 09.06.2018].

National Audit Office, 2008. *Department for Work and Pensions- Increasing Employment Rates for Ethnic Minorities*. Available at: https://www.nao.org.uk/wp-content/uploads/2008/02/0708206.pdf [Accessed 09.06.2018].

Pitcher, B., 2014. *Consuming Race*. London: Routledge:

Roethler, J., 1998. Reading in Color: Children's Book Illustrations and Identity Formation for Black Children in the United States. *African American Review*, 32 (1), 95–105.

Smith, A. and Lewis-Todd K., 2017. *Where Are the Black Dolls in High Street Stores?* BBC News. (2nd January 2017). Available at: https://www.bbc.co.uk/news/uk-england-nottinghamshire-38065205 [Accessed 12.06.2018].

Standards and Testing Agency, 2017. *Early Years Foundation Stage Profile 2018 Handbook*. Available at: https://assets.publishing.service.gov.uk/government/uploads/system/attachment_data/file/669079/Early_years_foundation_stage_profile_2018_handbook.pdf [Accessed 13.05.2018].

Swanson, D.P., Cunningham, M., Youngblood, J., and Spencer, M.B., 2009. *Racial Identity Development during Childhood*, pp 269–281. Available at: https://repository.upenn.edu/cgi/viewcontent.cgi?article=1203&context=gse_pubs [Accessed 03.03.2018].

Willis, G. and Lander, V., 2015. Why Do Mirrors Lie? *Race Equality Teaching*, 33 (2), 33–43.

Supporting communication via the outdoors

Moira Moran

OVERVIEW OF CHAPTER

This chapter explores the potential of the outdoor environment to encourage and enable children's communication. Using the "means, reasons and opportunities" communication model (Money and Thurman 2002) as a framework, the chapter analyses some of the "how", "why", and "when" aspects of communication from the child's perspective, linking these additionally to the practitioner's role in ensuring that each of these aspects is available and accessible to every child. As in other chapters of this book, the child is envisioned within Bronfenbrenner's ecological nested environments, and consequently consideration is given to the child's family and community contexts.

The chapter responds to the current interest in outdoor learning and development shared by an increasing number of early years settings. The influence of Scandinavian pedagogies is referenced within a broad interpretation of the United Kingdom Forest School ethos, and links are formed with theories of child development. This provides the reader with a range of key principles to support the provision of an enabling outdoor environment which is child centred, indeed often child led, and therefore rich in affordances for communication. The chapter discussion is underpinned by many vignettes from practice which vividly exemplify the impact of sensitive, empathetic practitioner actions in response to the perspective of the child and which offer the reader opportunities to reflect on their own practice and provision.

Introduction to the chapter

Earlier chapters have discussed the subject of communication as a basic human characteristic and a driver of children's development from birth. Article 19 of the Universal Declaration of Human Rights recognises communication as a basic human right, and the right and ability to communicate underpins many other human rights, in particular those of participation. Additionally, earlier chapters have raised the issue of the messages communicated to children by their environment and the extent to which they see themselves reflected and represented there (or not). Consequently, the contribution of the communication environment has been identified as key in identity formation, contributing significantly to children's well-being.

If we as practitioners working with children recognise that basic characteristic and right, and accept that communication is the channel between the individual child and the world around them, then it is clear that we also accept the responsibility to provide the most conducive environment possible to promote communication development. It is also a responsibility to ensure that the environment and the communications within it offer the child affirming experiences and messages, supporting positive image formation and wellbeing for all. This chapter will examine the special potential of the outdoor environment, different from that of the indoor, to contribute to children's development.

A well-established model and one frequently used when discussing the development of communication is the "means, reasons and opportunities" model (Money and Thurman 2002). When presented as circles of a Venn diagram, each element represented within a circle, the optimum environment for communication is at the centre where all circles intersect, and all elements are equally present.

Using the three supportive requisites of means, reasons, and opportunities, this chapter will interrogate the different possibilities of an outdoor environment to support children's communication development. The chapter will examine some of the challenges facing practitioners who want to take their teaching and children's learning outdoors. These challenges will be addressed through case studies, which draw on the rich affordances of the outdoor environment. Recent research is reviewed to support practitioners to reflect on their personal values for, and approaches to, children's learning. Models of social and constructivist pedagogy are offered for consideration and as possibilities for professional development.

The outdoor environment

For those working with young children, the term "outdoor environment" will conjure an image which differs from individual to individual, largely influenced by circumstances, experiences, emotions, and opportunities, both personal and professional. For some it will be a positive image of happy and engaged practitioners and children involved in stimulating experiences in an interesting and attractive setting; for others it is a less positive image with more mixed sensations.

For some the image conjured up will be of a Forest School session with its specific characteristics of child-led, open-ended experiences in a natural environment; for others the image may be of a more limited man-made space with an accompanying onus on the practitioners to provide variety and stimulation. And for many, it will be an image of somewhere in between. However, the significance of any outdoor environment is that it is different from the indoor. White (2011) describes the "special nature" including rich sensations, change and variety in natural elements, and the opportunity for children to follow their interests in an environment over which adults have less control than they have indoors. Wattchow and Brown (2011) cite Cameron who suggests that

> the task of the educator is how to foster an inclusive sense of place in students so that their love of wild places can extend to care for all places, even neglected city spaces.
>
> (2011, p. xxi)

The following example evidences all of White's special aspects within just such a small city space as Cameron refers to.

A BRIDGE FOR ANTS

Ben, Ari and Charlotte are playing outside in the small tarmac area of their nursery. The warm sunshine has brought out a column of ants and this has caught their interest. They crouch down to watch, and Ben runs to fetch three of the magnifying glasses which are continuously available outside. Jodi, an observant and interested practitioner and key person to Ben and Charlotte, joins the group. The ants are moving along a low brick wall, but the wall is broken, involving them in moving down to the playground to cross the gap before climbing back up to continue their progress along the wall. The four share previous experiences – a natural history programme about leafcutter ants, their recent topic on The 3 Billy Goats Gruff, crossing a stream on a fallen log on holiday – and resolve to help the ants by building a natural bridge. The discussion moves on to the length, thickness, strength of the twigs and stems they find, to the number and direction of the moving ants, to the potential impact of wind or rain on the bridge they have built. They agree that there should be 2 bridges, one for each direction of travel, and that they should be protected from the elements.

This example also provides some answers to the challenge of the nature of teaching and learning outdoors. All phases of education in the UK have identified outcomes for children to achieve, though these vary between the four countries. Planning, curriculum, assessment, and targets towards these outcomes can become a rigid rather than a supportive framework. Teaching can be understood and interpreted as adult planned and adult led. And yet, there is not an area of learning as identified in the Early Years Foundation Stage (EYFS) (DfE 2017) which these children and their responsive practitioner did not visit in their collaborative discussion. The verbal dialogue included the characteristics of sustained shared thinking and enabled the characteristics of effective learning (DfE 2017). Jodi recognised a teachable moment in the children's curiosity and developing exploration, cumulatively building on past and shared experience. She demonstrated the "in the moment" response referred to by Gripton in Chapter 5 which allowed thinking and communication to develop. The circumstances allowed Ben, Charlotte, and Jodi to draw on and strengthen the close key relationship they have formed throughout their time together in the setting, and to include Ari in it.

The outdoor environment has the possibility to be so much more than a playground for children, with adults attendant in a supervisory capacity concerned with ensuring safety and intervening in squabbles over turns on the "best" bike. Time spend outdoors is perceived by many as more than a "playtime" opportunity for children to let off steam, to use up physical energy before coming back inside to do the real work. Understandings of outdoor learning rest on the work of experiential theorists such as Rousseau, Dewey, and Bruner. The key role of the adult in learning is identified in the socio-cultural scaffolding theories of Vygotsky (the more knowledgeable other) and Rogoff (guided participation).

Increasingly the role of the place itself in children's learning is being understood. Jack (2010) advocates further attention should be given to attachment to *place* in addition to attachment to *people*, emphasising how linked and repeated direct experiences in a place support the formation of social ties. He suggests that "place, identity and well-being are often closely connected" (2010, p. 758) and that "feelings of belonging tend to be strongest amongst young people who perceive that they have been fully included and accepted within their local community" (ibid.).

Echoing Bronfenbrenner's ecological systems, Sobel (2004) was an early proponent of place-based education urging educators to find the learning potential in the local environment and community, viewing the active experiential learning possibilities as an alternative to the classroom and books. Grunewald (2008) describes ecological place-based education as having distinct characteristics, including

(a) it emerges from the particular attributes of place, (b) it is inherently multidisciplinary, (c) it is inherently experiential, (d) it is reflective of an

educational philosophy that is broader than "learning to earn", and (e) it connects place with self and community.

(2008, p. 314)

In their discussion of the pedagogy of place Wattchow and Brown (2011) concur

place refers to a participatory and experiential phenomenon. Our experience of a place is always a combination of a specific physical location, our embodied encounter and the cultural ideas that influence the interpretations we make of the experience.

(2011, p. ix)

There are many international models to support a pedagogic approach to outdoor learning, particularly in Scandinavian countries. Jordet (in Bentsen and Jensen 2012, p. 205) defined the pedagogy of Danish udeskole (outdoor school) as a sensory and experiential approach to learning which accentuates communication, social interaction, and play. Gelter (2000) describes the friluftsliv (free air life) philosophy of Sweden and Norway in its application to education emphasising the importance of well-being.

Friluftsliv may have the same ultimate goal as environmental education, but does not use any educational institution as educational aid, except nature itself... The overall goal for both would be a healthy soul in a healthy body in a healthy society in a healthy world, where respect and responsibility would be the new foundation of human interactions.

(Gelter 2000, p. 90)

Additionally and importantly, the outdoor environment can be seen as a neutral space for children's experiences, in a way that the indoor classroom frequently is not for all children. The following account exemplifies this feature. Janine is a Foundation Stage teacher in an inner-city school. Seven different languages are spoken by the children in her unit, so learning English is a high priority for many of her children. Every week, supported by as many adults as she can recruit from staff, parents, and volunteers, she and the children walk to a privately owned local woodland which has been made accessible to them for Forest School session. This is how Janine described the value of the session.

For many of the children in the Foundation Unit who do not speak English, the classroom is a bit of a mystery. While we make every effort to reflect their cultures in the classroom, through our signage, images and resources, our environment can be very different from their familiar one, and this can present a challenge on entry. They face an additional challenge with verbal communication, as the main language of the classroom is English, and the children's levels of comprehension and expression in English varies significantly.

When I began to bring the group to the woodland, I could not believe the difference for some of the children. The woodland is not used by the local community, so was a new space for everyone, and this immediately acted as a great leveller amongst the children. Within this neutral space, new heroes emerged, whether it is the bravest, the best climber, the fastest roly-poly-er or the best flower spotter. Children who struggled to make their place in the classroom, excelled in the new environment. Rather than sort of hovering on the edges, they became engrossed and more engaged than I usually saw them. And the best and most unexpected spin off from that has been the rise in confidence and the urge to share their new skills and experiences verbally. I constantly plan carefully for Communication and Language to support this particular group's development and so I have found I can use the woodland and our activities to teach key vocabulary that the children will need to talk about their experiences. I share this with the adults coming with me and we take advantage of every opportunity to use and reinforce the words in our conversations about what is going on. Then when we come back to the Unit we make books and displays of all the photographs I take, and we talk about it again. We have a slide show when the parents come to collect, we talk about it again. They have come to expect it on a Wednesday, and I know that when they go home, they talk about it again together as a family. The development of the children's language has been noticeable, and the confidence gained in the woodland has gradually come into classroom, enhancing social relationships, which in turn, enables more communication opportunities.

Janine's reflection proposes some important aspects of her children's experiences of the affordances of the outdoor environment. Her observation indicates children achieving Csikszentmihalyi's state of flow when "challenges and skill are in balance, attention becomes ordered and fully invested". (Csikszentmihalyi 1997, p. 38). Within the classroom she identified some children as having little of what Bourdieu's theory (1986) refers to as cultural capital, and therefore they are on the margins of the field. In the more neutral environment of the woodland a new set of valued skills, language, and tastes is co-constructed by the whole group, creating a more equitably shared cultural capital. Griffiths discusses enjoyment and engagement as an intrinsic to the experiences of a socially just education system,

I have argued that a socially just society aims to be one in which its members find a good life. I have also argued that educational experience is part of what it is to have a good life, at any age.

(Griffiths 2012, p. 666)

She proposes that the pedagogical relationship between child and teacher (Vygotsky would suggest a more knowledgeable other) plays a pivotal role in the educational experience.

Janine exemplifies for us how the enabling outdoor environment has become a rich space for her and her class, offering shared interests, shared language, and shared communication systems.

A means to communicate in the outdoor environment

In 2018 Stephen Hawking died. He was a Cambridge professor and a physicist with a string of letters after his name, many international prizes and a long list of publications. As a young man with progressive motor-neurone disease he lost the ability to speak and the ability to write by hand. Surprisingly, when reporting his death, many commentators celebrated his huge achievements and his impact on the world of science and knowledge while declaring that he had lost the ability to "communicate". As early years practitioners we are much too aware of the multitude of means of communication through which children express themselves to limit our thinking to children's speaking and handwriting. Amy was certainly aware, as the following example shows

LEXI AND THE FIRE STEEL

Lexi is attending her last in a series of forest school sessions and the group is about to light a fire and toast marshmallows as a finale. There is high excitement as a consequence. All the children are sitting in the log circle with a fire steel and a cotton ball each and are trying to light the ball with a spark, with varying success. But Lexi has a severe visual impairment and cannot see her steel or cotton ball clearly, and so is reluctant to try to make a spark. She tells Amy, her practitioner who has supported her engagement in the sessions and activities, that she is frightened that she won't see the fire and might burn herself. Amy tries to reassure Lexi that she will make sure she doesn't get hurt, but Lexi repeats that she can't see the fire, and is obviously dejected by her situation. Amy encourages her and they strike the steel together, Amy supporting Lexi hand-over-hand. When Lexi's spark lights the cotton ball, Amy gently asks "Can you smell it, Lexi? Can you smell the fire?" Lexi grins widely and shouts to her friends "I made a fire, look I made one too".

Here Lexi is communicating with the world around her using her sense of smell as effectively as her peers are using their sense of sight, supported by a sensitive practitioner who is responsive to her particular needs. Through acknowledging Lexi's ways of thinking and of speaking, Amy is modelling the "critical accept-ance and respect for [her] *as an individual*" referred to previously by Ulanowsky. This is paramount in the process of both Amy and Lexi's mindful recognition of her as a person, and critical to Lexi's positive concept of self.

This example brings to mind Malaguzzi's poem in which he proposes the hun-dred languages of children

> *The child has*
> *a hundred languages*
> *a hundred hands*
> *a hundred thoughts*
> *a hundred ways of thinking*
> *of playing, of speaking*

(Filippini and Vecchi 2000, p. 3)

Body language, gestures, tone of voice, and behaviour all communicate a child's levels of engagement and involvement to the observant and receptive adult. Often it takes a little longer to tune in to the non-verbal communications of children and a flexible outdoor session can allow time for communication in many forms.

A reason to communicate in the outdoor environment

Children must have a reason to communicate, without reason they have no need to, or there is no point in their doing so. Open-ended questions, sustained shared thinking, co-construction of learning, and genuinely interesting experiences all offer the rich communication possibilities that can encourage children's commu-nication, whether non-verbal or verbal.

Rosa provides an example of this:

ROSA AND THE CAMPFIRE

Rosa enjoys the sessions when the preschool children use the small woodland in the corner of the nursery garden. She is happy to go, and always keen to tell her dad what she has been doing when he picks her up. She is small for her age, and a little hesitant in her approach to the physical challenges. She likes to sit quietly and at these times appears to be absorbing the environment through her senses, running her fingers over the place she is sitting, hearing birds, and turning her face to the weather; sun, wind, or rain. But when it is time to set the fire, a different Rosa emerges. From experience, she

(continued)

(continued)

knows this is a task best achieved as a team, so she gathers a community of practice around herself and, using shared goals and language, she confidently leads the enterprise, directing the collection and sorting of sticks, sending out for more kindling and instructing the building of an effective fire. Her father reports that she "bosses" the family similarly in the garden at the weekend, sending her older brother and parents around the garden where grass stands for sticks, and buttercups and daisies are kindling.

Nicholson (1971 in Woods 2017) posits a theory of Loose Parts, hypothesising

In any environment, both the degree of inventiveness and creativity, and the possibility of discovery, are directly proportional to the number and kinds of variables.

(Woods 2017, p. 110)

Here, Rosa is using her knowledge, skills, and understanding of real fire lighting with real loose parts and applying it to the loose parts of her own garden with inventiveness and creativity. The natural objects in both settings foster the flexibility of her thinking which is exemplified in that process. She is using the vocabulary of the woodland session to transfer her knowledge and skills as a more knowledgeable other, taking the lead role in guiding the participation of her less knowledgeable family. We can surmise that as a young and physically small member of the group, and the youngest in the family, she is finding the role of leader to be a positive one. Her mastery of setting a fire is affording Rosa the opportunity to add to the bi-directional skein of communication between her circles of influence which Bronfenbrenner emphasised as critical for the child's well-being. This combination of circumstances gives her the reason to give information, express her feelings, and voice her choices.

Some children find verbal communication more difficult than others for a variety of reasons. A Forest School leader shares her experience.

KAYDEN THE WIZARD

A local school was bringing the children from Nurture Group to the site for a series of sessions. In conversation beforehand we were told that one boy did not speak at school, though he displayed good understanding of English, did join activities, and could follow instructions. When the group arrived for the first session, the staff told us that Kayden had needed a lot of support and encouragement to come, and they were not sure they would get him through the door to the gathering room, but they eventually had done so.

We set off to the site, and started the session as usual. We unobtrusively observed Kayden join in the activities pretty quickly. His support assistant responded by gradually drawing back from him, allowing him the autonomy he was telling us he wanted. He chose to whittle a stick with my colleague Colin, and while sitting on his log whittling he started to sing quietly.

On the second session Kayden strode confidently into the room and made a bee-line to sit next to Colin. That week Colin was mixing magic potions and Kayden chose that activity to join. Kayden adapted the activity, and using his mixing wand he put a spell on Colin, and shouted "1, 2, 3, freeze!" as he did so. Over and over again! No sooner had he "unfrozen" Colin than he froze him again.

We pondered on this after the session, trying to figure out what had enabled this change in Kayden. He was certainly enjoying Colin's company, and the nature of the freeze game certainly made sure he had Colin's attention. But we also felt that Kayden was sharing an interest with Colin and that the to and fro of freeze and un-freeze was a type of dialogue to maintain and sustain the sharing.

The example demonstrates how Kayden had found a reason in these sessions to use verbal communication. The staff had reported that he did not speak in school (importantly, not that he *could not* speak) and had never heard him sing. Obviously he had listened to the singing and knew the words, and through the known song he first made his voice heard in the session. Having done that, his second step was a more independent one, where he chose to use speech to express his choices and his desire to establish a relationship, a new way of being with Colin and retaining his attention. This was undoubtedly facilitated by the higher adult/child ratio in a Forest School session than in a classroom. These were significant steps in Kayden's communication and staff reported that gradually and over time he found reasons to talk at school.

Opportunities to communicate in the outdoor environment

Waite (2011, p. 79) identifies practitioner values for outdoor learning to be "freedom, fun, authenticity, autonomy and physicality", resulting in a move from the traditional classroom-based directive pedagogy to more creative pedagogies of co-construction

The child-initiated play-based affordances of outdoor learning enable the wide variety of opportunities by which children communicate their interests and ideas to each other and to practitioners who watch and listen carefully. In a small-scale study with Welsh Foundation Phase teachers engaged in Reggio-style projects, Waters and Maynard (2010) discovered a significant difference between aspects of activity and practice indoors and outdoors. They measured the subject of child-initiated communications in a flexible outdoor environment, finding "loose parts…, features of landscape/being…, (and) wildlife" (2010, p. 478) to be the elements of outdoor provision which most often prompted children's discussion with adults. With Clement they further identified (Maynard et al. 2013) that, although many activities were *teacher initiated* both indoors and out, outdoors the number of activities in which the subsequent direction of the activity was *led by the child* was considerably higher. Likewise, outdoors teachers acted more frequently as facilitator/supporter than indoors, where they took on the role of instructor the majority of the time. Teacher interactions were principally open outdoors, and principally closed indoors.

When practitioners recognise the rich potential of the outdoor environment as a communication friendly space they can capitalise on opportunities as they arise. Many early years settings adopt a free-flow approach to their sessions, which allows staff to follow the children indoor or out, ensuring that there are always sufficient adults to interact with the children in their interests and fascinations. In the case of the increasing numbers of settings which offer Forest School sessions to their children, then the likelihood is that the adult to child ratio will be high, as recommended by the Forest School Association (FSA) (Forest School Association. no date). These circumstances offer the optimum opportunity for engagement with children in a paired and partnership approach to their motivating experiences and in dialogic discussions which support the child's proximal development (Waller 2014).

Scandinavian colleagues have talked of their approach to the outdoor natural environment as allowing occasions for "being in a place; not doing in a place", like Rosa when absorbing the elements. With fewer adult learning outcomes set prior to the session, there is time to slow down, to take time, and to allow children to lead in a direction that interests them. Sometimes there is time to do very little, to just "be" and we have all witnessed those moments when children stop and appear to be doing nothing, perhaps staring closely or into the distance, adopting a calm and stillness which is not their usual way. Sometimes it is a moment of awe or wonder which stops them in their tracks and absorbs their attention completely, as described here by a practitioner:

It is some weeks since we have visited our Forest School site, for a variety of reasons. As we get close, we turn a bend and are faced by a long, wide, walk, absolutely carpeted in tall white ox-eye daisies, and sloping uphill as far as we can see. They were not there at our last visit and, at around a metre tall, these are bigger than some of the children. We are all stopped in our tracks, there are some sharp intakes of breath, and for a moment no one says a word. Then one child whispers "look, look" as if scared that if we make too much noise they will disappear again. We stay there for a long time, talking quietly about the phenomenon, musing on how it happened when we weren't there, and moving carefully round the edges so no one steps on a single flower. There is a hush and a general feeling of respect for this natural environment, which is also discussed. As some children are ready, they move on in small groups with a practitioner, but it is a long time till the last group has finished their discussion and is ready to move on.

This is an example of dialogue based on collaboration in shared experience between adults and children. In this occasion, the awe and wonder were genuinely and collectively felt and led to a sustained and wide-ranging reciprocal discussion which could not have been planned for. Again, our Scandinavian colleagues have a saying which reflects the situation: "Sometimes we walk in front of the children, sometimes we walk with them, and sometimes we walk behind". It is a skilled practitioner who always knows their place! We all get it wrong sometimes, but the particular nature of the outdoor environment and children's interactions within it can grant us permission to be flexible in our role.

Conclusion

An element of Moon's (1999) discussion of reflection identifies it as a "gentle process" and "state of mind" (1999, p. 60) which can include emotion and intuition. In that context it may be useful to reflect on personal environments for communication.

When are our personal means, reasons, and opportunities optimally present? Do we always communicate verbally or are different means of communication used? Dancers communicate with each other and with their audience without words; authors are involved in a solitary process until their work emerges in print to communicate to their reader; an art group may meet at a gallery, inspired to sketch and discuss their work.

Where do we feel most comfortable to communicate? For me it can be meeting an old friend for a quiet country walk, reminiscing on our shared experiences and swapping news of family and mutual friends. We can all think of environments which are not as conducive to communication. For those who most often chat at the kitchen table over a cup of tea, conversation may not be the same or flow so freely in a formal restaurant with an attentive waiter hovering nearby.

The same is true for children. Laevers wrote "'Like a fish in water' - that is how you can describe children who feel alright". (2005, p. 7). We must acknowledge that the outdoor environment is not the most comfortable for all children. There will be a variety of reasons for this: unfamiliarity, anxiety, dislike of certain elements, even phobia in some cases. For many children more positive responses develop through their own participation and through the role models of their engaged peers and enthusiastic adults, for others more thoughtful or targeted individual support is necessary. Our skill lies in working with children to overcome their barriers so that they can all "feel alright".

The element common to all successful communications is the innate urge to communicate and this personal reflection on our individual communication environment may support us in providing environments for all our children where they feel alright and their communication will thrive. It may help us to answer the question also asked by Gripton in Chapter 3: "what is it like to be a child here?" Again, (Moran 2015, p. 123) I refer to Malaguzzi's declaration,

> Stand aside for a while and leave room for learning, observe carefully what children do, and then, if you have understood well, perhaps teaching will be different from before.
>
> (1998, p. 82)

and suggest that observation plays a key part in ensuring our provision supports the communication needs of all children. Again I refer to our Scandinavian colleagues who say, "Sometimes we walk in front of the children, sometimes we walk with them, and sometimes we walk behind", and suggest that this approach can inform our decision as to the nature of our dialogues.

PROVOCATIONS

- The chapter has addressed the proposal that well-being and a sense of belonging are prerequisites to successful communication for children. How can this be nurtured for all our children in the outdoor environment?

- As practitioners working with children, we are mindful of the importance for young children of strong attachments to the people who care for them. Should we also give attention to place attachment, outdoors as well as in, and how can we support this for children?

- Our practice, and therefore that of the setting, is influenced by our personal views and values. This chapter has asked you to reflect on the outdoors as a communication enabling environment. What are the views and values of the wider team on this question, and do you all agree?

References

Bentsen, P. and Jensen, F., 2012. The Nature of Udeskole: Outdoor learning theory and practice in Danish schools. *Journal of Adventure Education & Outdoor Learning*, 12 (3), 199–219.

Bourdieu, P., 1986. The Forms of Capital. In I. Szeman, and T. Kaposy, eds. *Cultural Theory: An anthology*. Oxford: Wiley & Sons, 2011, 81–97.

Csikszentmihalyi, M., 1997. *Finding Flow: The psychology of engagement with everyday life*. New York: Basic Books.

Department for Education, 2017. *Early Years Foundation Stage Statutory Framework (EYFS)*. Available at: https://www.gov.uk/government/publications/early-years-foundation-stage-framework--2 [Accessed 27.03.2018].

Forest School Association. No date. *Principles and Criteria for Good Practice*. Available at: https://www.forestschoolassociation.org/full-principles-and-criteria-for-good-practice [Accessed 25.05.2018].

Filippini, T. and Vecchi, V., eds., 2000. *The Hundred Languages of Children*. 3rd ed. Reggio Emilia: Reggio Children.

Gelter, H., 2000. Friluftsliv: The Scandinavian Philosophy of Outdoor Life. *Canadian Journal of Environmental Education*, 5 (1), 77–92.

Griffiths, M., 2012. Why Joy in Education Is an Issue for Socially Just Policies. *Journal of Education Policy*, 27 (5), 655–670.

Gruenewald, D., 2008. The Best of Both Worlds: A critical pedagogy of place. *Environmental Education Research*, 14 (3), 308–324.

Jack, G., 2010. Place Matters: The significance of place attachments for children's well-being. *The British Journal of Social Work*, 40 (3), 755–771.

Laevers, F., ed., 2005. *Well-being and Involvement in Care A Process-oriented Self-evaluation Instrument for Care Setting*. Leuven: Kind & Gezin and Research Centre for Experiential Education.

Malaguzzi, L., 1998. History, Ideas, and Basic Philosophy: An interview with Lella Gandini. In C. Edwards, L. Gandini, and G. Forman eds. *The Hundred Languages of Children: The Reggio Emilia approach—Advanced reflections*. Greenwich, CT: Ablex, 1998, 2nd ed., pp. 49–97.

Maynard, T., Waters, J., and Clement, J., 2013. Moving Outdoors: Further explorations of 'child-initiated' learning in the outdoor environment. *Education 3–13*, 41 (3), 282–299.

Money, D. and Thurman, S., 2002. *Inclusive Communication. Speech and Language Therapy in Practice*. London: Whurr.

Moran, M., 2015. Capturing the Possibilities. In A. Woods, ed. *The Characteristics of Effective Learning: Creating and capturing the possibilities in the early years*. London: Taylor & Francis, 2014, pp. 122–137.

Moon, J., 1999. *Reflection in Learning and Professional Development: Theory and practice*. London: Routledge.

Sobel, D., 2004. *Place-based Education: Connecting classrooms & communities*. Massachusetts: Orion Society.

Waite, S., 2011. Teaching and Learning Outside the Classroom: Personal values, alternative pedagogies and standards. *Education 3–13*, 39 (1), 65–82.

Waller, T., 2014. Voices in the Park: Researching the participation of young children in outdoor play in early years settings. *Management in Education*, 28 (4), 161–166.

Waters, J. and Maynard, T., 2010. What's so Interesting Outside? A study of child-initiated interaction with teachers in the natural outdoor environment. *European Early Childhood Education Research Journal*, 18 (4), 473–483.

Wattchow, B. and Brown, M., 2011. *A Pedagogy of Place: Outdoor education for a changing world*. Victoria: Monash University Publishing.

White, J., 2011. Capturing the Difference: The special nature of the outdoors. In J. White, ed. *Outdoor Provision in the Early Years*. London: Sage, 2011, pp. 45–57.

Woods, A., 2017. *Elemental Play and Outdoor Learning: Young children's playful connections with people, places and things*. London: Routledge.

9 Digital media in early years settings

Helen Cazaly

OVERVIEW OF CHAPTER

This chapter will explore the development and use of digital communication systems in use in early years settings and consider them in line with the developing children's rights agenda relating to the ownership, use, and storage of digital information relating to children. Within this discussion there will also be a consideration of the use of digital media used by parents when mediating a child's world and the issues related to digital imagery and ownership of material. This will be linked to Bronfenbrenner's Ecological Systems Model (1979) by consideration of the role of digital media within a child's cultural world and how this forms a significant part of the macro system of a contemporary childhood.

While more settings are moving towards use of online communication and e-learning journey systems there is an expectation that all parents have internet access and that records will be accessible via digital media platforms in order to develop the communication pathways with parents. Working closely with parents and sharing information about their child's development is a key component in the current Ofsted inspection framework while there is a firm move away from the previous onerous requirements of detailed paper documentation in the form of learning journeys within the current incarnation of the Early Years Foundation Stage statutory framework (EYFS) (Department for Education 2017).

Consideration of the communications issues surrounding harder to reach parents, such as those with English as an additional language or without any English, when accessing these new forms of communication tools will also come under discussion throughout the chapter. Issues surrounding the data protection implications for storage of digital information and imagery as each setting becomes a Registered Data Controller under new data protection regulations recently introduced will also be introduced as a relevant contemporary area of practice.

(continued)

(continued)

There will also be a discussion of the implications relating to the software management and staff development programmes in order to ensure that these systems are being used safely and to their full potential as well as considering the implications of varied age ranges of staff members having differing attitudes and levels of safety awareness of social media use and platforms. A discussion around the responsibilities attached to the setting to teach e-safety to children and parents will also be included.

Introduction

Bronfenbrenner's Ecological Systems Model (1979) clearly demonstrates how all layers have a direct or indirect, overlapping impact upon a child's experience. The macro system includes the dominating culture within which the child's world exists. While this culture may more usually be considered as religious, ethical, or class, it can also be considered as being related to structural differences and experiences that can be reflected in a setting's local policies as well as in government initiatives. It does however become an important aspect of any consideration of communication with children to examine the way we communicate using alternative systems, by use of technology that may send a clear message to a child about their role in life, their personal value, and their ownership of their identity. These messages can be sent unintentionally but are received by the child regardless of intent. Cultural changes across time mean that adults reflecting back on their own experience of childhood and what impact cultural aspects may have had in order to improve a contemporary childhood experiences, may miss technological developments which have significantly changed the way we communicate with each other, with children, and about children. This is, therefore, a form of communication that sends a clear message to a child about their place in the world and our value of their emerging identities.

We exist increasingly in a digital world. We are awoken by digital alarms, either in clock format or on our mobile phones; listen to early morning digital radio signals or watch digital television. We check our emails, our social media news feeds and news websites to catch up with the overnight happenings of the world. All this happens before we leave the home to start our day. We are connected to the world in a way previous generations could not have imagined and, mostly, these digital communication systems are beneficial and used responsibly to enhance lives at all ages and stages. Many families have regular video calls to keep in touch across generations and continents giving children familial awareness and the opportunity to develop relationships with grandparents or extended family.

Children's digital awareness, therefore, is ingrained long before we, as practitioners, meet them in our early years settings and are able to exert influence on their digital media learning journey. A pictorial trail of their lives, often from pre-natal scan photo stage onwards, is spread across the worldwide web as parents and families share the celebration of these newly emerging humans. This is a trail which is then added to by documenting their developmental milestones and learning journeys by parents and practitioners throughout their early years and then beyond through to adulthood. Retailers actively encourage this culture by selling a wide range of "baby milestone", or achievement cards, which have largely taken the place of the traditional baby book where children's "firsts" were recorded before the digital age. Contemporary parenting now has a new form of memory saving and nostalgia to look back on, where the firsts (first smile, first tooth, first steps, etc.) are photographed alongside a decorated card with the achievement and date. These photographs are then uploaded to social media or emailed in order to share the first with family and friends. This practice adds to the digital footprint that starts with sharing a scan image and contributes to the developing cultural expectation that children's lives will be digitally documented and stored in the world of the internet.

Digital media use in early years settings

The rise of digital media use within the population as a whole is, not surprisingly, reflected in technological, management, and system changes in early years settings. This is not only within the management of records and data relating to the general day-to-day running of these business, but also as a tool to enhance communication and liaison with parents as well as information recording and sharing between settings where appropriate.

The rise of online software packages, or applications (apps) for more mobile technology, such as Tapestry™ or Kinderley™, which aim to provide a comprehensive way of recording photographs, observations and planning for each child have seen a large increase in use. More and more systems are being used and developed by all types of early years settings that can be shared with parents, but also retained as a virtual learning journey that will meet requirements for holding records on each child's development and achievements detailed in the EYFS.

The EYFS requires settings to keep a record of a child's developmental journey. In past incarnations of the EYFS, this has required a learning journey document to be kept which consists of images and observations mapped to developmentally appropriate learning outcomes and potential next planning steps for each child. This learning journey is also intended to be shared with parents, and as such, parents were invited to contribute with home observations and photographs in order to develop the essential parent partnership that we know enhances a child's experience in an early years setting. While the learning journey document itself is no longer statutory, settings are still required to be able to maintain a record of each child's development, which, in this digital age, has developed to become an online storage system involving the same capturing of moments through photographs and observations. Parents are able to gain access to these online software systems remotely by use of a password and indeed, some settings have web camera access to the setting accessible to parents throughout their opening hours to enable constant monitoring of their child's day. Parents are also invited to contribute to these online records with details of the child's home experiences as they would have done previously to a physical learning journey record.

Such software packages aim to provide, within one tool, everything a setting needs with features such as care diaries, the ability to share photographs with parents in "real time" (as they are taken), learning and development journeys, baseline assessments as well as features such as webinars (online seminar learning sessions), the ability to allow access to other relatives of the child to view certain features of that child's record, as well as invoicing and accounts options (dependent on the package in use). As such they are proving a very popular option across thousands of early years settings as the reduction in time consuming physical record keeping while creating a professional document that can be adapted to include a two-way flow of information from parents, carers, and other adults in a child's life with the potential of downloading the record as a permanent souvenir of the child's early years experiences.

This has been a welcome development by parents as well as settings. The majority of the current new generation of parents are "digital natives" (Prensky 2001). Their worlds have always been rooted in the digital technology of the worldwide web and smart phones. They cannot conceive of a time when a camera was not freely available in everyone's pocket, by way of their smart phone, or a time when the information superhighway did not exist – or even that it did not operate at superfast fibre-optic speeds or through 4G phone networks (which could be 5G by the time this goes to print!). For these parents as well as younger practitioners within early years settings, instant photography and social media is their lived normality and these online communication systems seem a natural and welcome progression in order to maintain contact and awareness of their child's day. The consideration of the 'digital footprint' left behind, however, is not always a major concern.

The child's 'digital footprint'

A 'digital footprint' is widely considered to be the trail that a person leaves behind following their internet usage. For adults and older children this would include emails sent and received, websites visited and forums contributed to amidst a wealth of other ways information is now stored about a person's online use. This does however give rise to the issue of how much of a digital footprint are adults creating on behalf of children in the early years in order to document their lives and improve communications with parents. With widespread use of social media sites, such as Facebook, Instagram, Twitter, and Snapchat (to name only a few), by parents, to share aspects of their lives (and their children's) with friends and family, as well as by businesses, such as early years settings, to promote their services, the trend for photo sharing and information sharing to a wider audience seems unstoppable. However, the impact on the child's digital footprint should now be considered very carefully from a moral and ethical position but also from a children's rights perspective.

There is a current, widespread concern about digital image use and storage by children and about children within our (still developing) rights-based society. The Children's Commissioner, Anne Longfield, has raised this issue clearly with the comment: "Most children no longer see a distinction between online and offline life. For most it is just life". (Longfield 2017). Her office is leading a drive towards considering how to improve the role and responsibilities of social media companies and parents as well as the government. While this is clearly targeted at the concerns surrounding older children, these issues become a lived normality within the early years as parents happily share images of their growing child on social media platforms such as Facebook, Instagram, and YouTube. While there appears to be a clear awareness of the types of image it is appropriate to upload by parents (bath time and beach pictures commonly have little smiley face 'emojis' added to give the child supposed modesty) there is also a wealth of early years settings happily sharing day-to-day images of their settings online through their business pages on social media platforms. While parents do have to have given consent to this sharing, it does raise the question and open a debate as to the ownership of the imagery used and the information held digitally on each child as they progress through early years settings and beyond. This debate is to be had not only over images and information shared on social media platforms but also those of the child's development record maintained through the previously discussed online packages aimed to improve communication. While it is perfectly acceptable to share images of children with prior parental consent, there is also a concern that these images can be easily downloaded and shared again by the parents or other visitors to the social media platform, effectively removing any control of the images the setting may have believed itself to have.

This falls within current wider concerns about the selling and passing on of data and personal information that has arisen recently with cases such as analytics companies harvesting data from social media platforms in order to target advertising to individuals and potentially change their behaviours. This creates a real concern about the amount and content of information sharing within the online world. This is an ongoing debate that may well affect future information sharing practices but early years settings have already released a torrent of images and information to the internet, over which they no longer have control.

Even more concerning is the child voice around the issues of 'sharenting' – when parents share images of their children online. Older children have been quite clear in their concerns and embarrassment about their parents' online shar-ing behaviours (Children's Commissioner's Office 2018). From a safeguarding per-spective, parents' images shared online often give away vital information about a child's location, home address, school or early years setting, introducing issues which are taught to older children as internet safety once they reach primary school but are not always immediately apparent to parents when considering their own digital practice.

Further concerns have been raised about the security of future generations when all the standard security questions (name of first school, name of first pet, mother's maiden name, etc.) have been happily shared online throughout a childhood. As practitioners we have to have serious consideration of our role in supporting parents with accurate advice in this area without taking the joy of parenting and sharing children's milestones away from them, at the same time as acknowledging that we do live in a digital world and a blanket ban on digital imagery use is not a sustainable way forward.

The legal position and ethical responsibilities

With the new EU General Data Protection Guidelines (GDPR) (European Union, 2016/679) replacing the old Data Protection Act of 1998 the issues around owner-ship of imagery have never been more relevant. Article 17 clearly states that an individual has the right to erasure of personal data (including images) pertain-ing to themselves. This is most commonly known as the "right to be forgotten". The Children's Commissioner is pushing hard for ownership of all imagery to be with the child and with an emphasis on the digital footprint rights of a child to have all online imagery removed on request once they are 18. While this would seem to be a very sensible and laudable development given the implications of ill-advised images of teenagers' social media and early relationship experiences, there also comes a consideration of the rights of the child when one turns to the issues attached to the development of the role of digital communication and imagery within early years settings. There is a very real danger that for the cur-rent generation, every child's developmental milestone will have been digitally stored with the potential for that image to be downloaded and shared without the consent of the child or parents at any point in the future. Although once the domain of jocular threats by parents to show baby photos to potential new part-ners, there is now the very real possibility that a person's baby photo could reap-pear anywhere, at any time. So without wishing to descend into issues attached to the online security of such software packages, there also would appear to be other issues attached to the widespread use of digital technology such as com-munication with parents becoming digitalised and the issues surrounding the ownership of each image of the child. There is a clear case for considering digital imagery with the same protectionist outlook as we do with accident and incident logs and paperwork where they are retained until each child reaches 21 years and three months in order to have a document trail in cases of a young adult wanting to pursue a claim against a setting in later years.

CASE STUDY

Jennifer has worked hard to develop her daycare nursery, Little Monkeys, in a small town. She has embraced digital technology and used Facebook to promote the business and encourage parents to take up their child's funded nursery hours at Little Monkeys. She is particularly proud of the outdoor space the children have open access to all year round and has taken a range of photos in all weathers showing the children having fun, playing and learning, in the outdoor environment. All parents give consent (or withhold consent) for imagery to be used within the child's records as well as separate consent for use of imagery to promote the business. Jennifer is scrupulous in ensuring only images with consent are ever shared on the business Facebook page.

One of Jennifer's staff members, Kayleigh, has lived in the small town all her life and as a result knows a lot of the parents on an informal basis outside of the work environment, having been to school with many of them. Kayleigh is an active Facebook user and is "friends" with over 800 other users, many of which are current or past parents in the setting. Kayleigh raises concerns with Jennifer that a parent of a child who left last summer to start at the local primary school appears to be sharing images of the child in the outdoor space of Little Monkeys. On checking, Jennifer discovers that these are indeed images that were shared over a year ago to promote the opening of the forest school area of the outdoor space. There is nothing inappropriate about the photograph but Jennifer is aware that she has now clearly lost control of that image as it can be downloaded and shared by anyone with access to the parent's profile.

■ Jennifer decides to review all policies relating to information sharing to include those of child images as well as create a written Social Media Policy for her staff that makes it clear what expectations of professionalism the setting has when staff use social media platforms.

■ A parents' evening is planned in order to help develop parental understanding of the safety implications of sharing images of their children widely online as well as helping them to review their security setting within their social media platforms.

■ Jennifer is now aware of the ethical issues attached to sharing images online and will revise the setting's approach to ownership of child images.

Accessibility issues associated with e-learning journey systems

A lot of the work undertaken to develop digital formats for early years settings to record children's progress has been with a view to improving and developing communication with the more hard-to-reach parents such as working parents or non-resident parents. Although many of these formats offer the opportunity of a two-way flow of communication between the child's main carers and the setting there remain concerns around the viability of this within the context of parents who may not have English as their first language or those struggling parents, for whom face-to-face communication about the child also becomes a form of support and advice for parenting. There are also issues attached to the access of the more disadvantaged families to relevant technology to be able to make full use of the digital opportunities this could offer. Within all these packages, there is an assumption that the parents have constant access to the internet and the technological know-how to be able to develop their use of the package. While this may well be the case for the majority of parents it does raise questions as to how difficult this may become for a parent for whom English is not their first language or who may not have acquired any written English skills to be able to access the formats.

Bronfenbrenner's (1979) Ecological Systems Model suggests that communication between various components of a child's individual system (the meso-sytem) should be of benefit to the child's experience but little research has been undertaken into whether this should take the form of face-to-face communication or whether digital formats are equally valuable. When compared with the old 'satchel post' system of sending information home, these new systems do appear, at first glance, to be more viable and accessible. However, when considering the information sent in the context of the six steps of Argyle's (1972) Communication Cycle (Figure 9.1) there are several potential disruptions to the cycle when considering it in the context of information sharing from an early years setting to a parent or carer.

The first potential issue can occur at the "message coded" and "message decoded" stages (2 and 5). In today's multicultural and multilingual society how can a setting know that their "message" or communication is going to be easily read and understood by the intended recipient (the parent)? Even within an English-speaking household, sending communication by any form other than direct face-to-face contact, assumes a level of literacy that, sadly, not all adults have. A setting has to ensure that they are aware of all home languages, literacy, and competency in English or home language. It is not uncommon for a setting to translate all newsletters and emails into home languages only to find that the recipients are not literate.

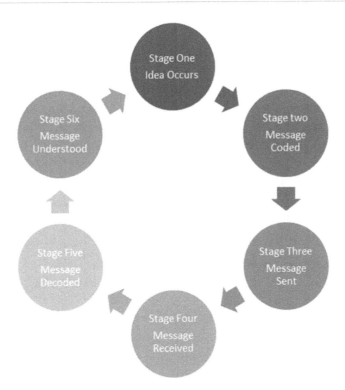

Figure 9.1 Argyle's communication cycle

The second potential issue could be at the "message sent" and "message received" stages (3 and 4). If sending communications by text, email, or via an online journal platform, there is the immediate assumption that the recipient has access to, and checks, their receiving systems on a regular basis. With digital native staff in a setting, it may be inconceivable that a parent does not check their digital devices several times a day and yet there is still a large part of the population that treat email like the postal service – a quick look in the mail box once a day (or less frequently). There is also an assumption at this stage that the recipient has constant internet connectivity which, again, is not always the case as there are financial costs associated with internet access as well as issues surrounding mobile signal "black spots" and broadband access in some parts of the country.

Beyond these language, literacy, and access issues there remain the issues around the "message understood" stage (6). Practitioners referring to learning areas of the EYFS, early learning goals, developmental milestones for example, all have the potential for a parent or carer to not understand the everyday language (or jargon) of an early years setting. This has been highlighted as a clear barrier to encouraging parental involvement in developing a child's learning journey book and many settings now run face-to-face sessions to advise parents what the EYFS entails and how they incorporate that into a child's day.

Incorporating e-safety into our planning and delivery for all children

This leads to a discussion of how to communicate with very young children about digital safety, imagery and use within a world where we know that they will have to become competent users of technology even before primary school transitions.

The EYFS has a clear message that technology is a part of childhood:

Early Learning Goal 15 Technology:

- Children recognise that a range of technology is used in places such as homes and schools
- They select and use technology for particular purposes
                                        (Standards and Testing Agency 2017)

Although the early learning goals are under review this aspect of children's early learning is unlikely to change given the digital world they inhabit. This gives practitioners a responsibility to communicate with children about their own safety and the safety of others when using technology of all kinds in exactly the same way we communicate all other aspects of encouraging children to take responsibility for their own safety.

The recent "Life in 'likes'" (Children's Commissioner's Office 2018) research with older children demonstrates that children are well aware of the logos associated with mobile phone apps from ages far younger than they are legally able to open their own account. Parents pass their phones to children to use the associated games and cameras, and to enable them to view video content, which is routinely seen as a way of keeping them occupied as a regular, daily event in many children's lives, as any bus or train journey or time spent in a GP surgery waiting room can demonstrate. This is supported by Pan-European research on the technology use of children under 5 which highlighted that children are "digitally fluent" users of technology from very young ages (Palaiologou 2014) with findings from the same study concluding that early years settings need to develop their environments and systems of working to incorporate this newly emerging aspect of early childhood.

In contrast, within early years settings we have strict guidelines on the access to, and use of, mobile phones during the working day as a result of major safeguarding breakdowns previously experienced within the sector. Although many role play areas have old mobile phones to encourage language and appropriate use of technology, it would be very rare to find a setting where there is a connected mobile for children to learn about safe use of cameras, apps, and internet but this is increasingly an essential tool for the new generation to navigate their way through their future worlds.

There is a clear role, and need, for communicating about e-safety to very young children in order to empower them in the digital world. Communication surrounding issues such as people not always being who they appear online can have parallels with age old stories such as Little Red Riding Hood and online bullying has parallels with The Three Little Pigs, or the Billy Goats Gruff. Early years practitioners already have a wealth of adaptable stories at their fingertips to be able to explore and communicate around safe digital technology use with very young children. We are comfortable promoting safeguarding concepts such as the NSPCC PANTS campaign that stipulates a child's body is theirs and theirs alone, so should we not also be communicating to children that digital images of themselves are also theirs now, as well as once they turn 18? This does leave the rather uncomfortable realisation however, that in the same way that we have to explore difficult issues around safeguarding that entail an implicit explanation to children that there is danger in their world, we now have to generate a new level of communication around how to keep themselves safe online at the same time as the very early ages that they begin to use technology, rather than leave it until the National Curriculum considers it an appropriate subject to include in the school experience. Although there are strong calls to strengthen the teaching of e-safety in schools (NSPCC 2018) the potential to start this learning within early years is still largely unexplored within the literature.

Implications for the future

When we consider very young children in the sensori-motor stage (Piaget, 1936), happily using touch screen tablets and phones without any difficulty or frustrations the position becomes even clearer. Our very youngest children are very often being exposed to this technology without adequate adult awareness of the further implications. While there is a vocal body of professionals who consider all technology inappropriate for young children, there is a challenge to this approach by considering that as reflective practitioners we cannot ignore the developing digital world for children by not adequately addressing this in our planning and resourcing of settings. We have to accept a level of responsibility in developing this aspect of a child's learning and life experiences with the acknowledgement that the early years setting is a training ground for later childhood and adult behaviours.

With this in mind, we have to consider that without adapting our approach we are moving towards a situation similar to that of children's nutrition where we are teaching healthy diet and lifestyles as part of the Personal, Social, and Emotional Development prime area of learning in the EYFS but then sending children home to families where, potentially, their nutritional subject knowledge is not adequate to support what the children have learned within the setting and the child's home diet remains unhealthy. If we consider the issues surrounding technology under discussion within this chapter as a 'Digital Diet and Lifestyle' equivalent we are in a similar position in as much as, the children arrive with us with preconceived ideas and experiences of acceptable use of technology without the consideration of personal safety or future impact as their previous experience has been shaped by parental use and sharing practices.

We need careful consideration right now, and not in future generations, of the best practice to enhance safe use of technology at the same time as teaching responsible ownership of imagery to adults or we potentially face the digital equivalent of the current childhood obesity crisis.

Chapter summary

Within a child's early years all aspects of their environment contribute to their personal development and identity construction. Developing an ethical practice model for all early years settings that includes an awareness that the child's body is their own – which includes all digital imagery of that body too – is the clearest, right's defined, way forward for all people working with children. Systems and policies must be developed that protect the child as well as the setting against future claims of bad practice regarding image sharing. Parents who engage with online e-learning journey systems need to be given clear guidance on the imagery and information shared with them from a protectionist standpoint while encouraging them to celebrate their child's life and achievements.

This chapter has opened a discussion surrounding the use of digital media as a communication tool rather than providing solutions to potential issues of this developing platform within the early years sector. It is hoped the reader will consider their own sharing practices as well as those of their setting and consider the child's "right to be forgotten" as much as other issues within the child rights agenda.

PROVOCATIONS

- How, in this digital world, do we communicate with parents about their child's learning experience at the same time as encouraging them to consider safe internet sharing practices themselves?

- How do we then communicate this to the children themselves, without criticising their parents' behaviours, while maintaining the child right's perspective that ownership of that imagery is the child's not ours?

(continued)

(continued)

■ How do we develop our storage and control of digital imagery in order to ensure that images are not misappropriated and that we can adhere to a child's right "to be forgotten" in later years?

References

Argyle, M., 1972, *The Psychology of Interpersonal Behaviour.* 2nd ed. Harmondsworth: Pelican.

Bronfenbrenner, U., 1979, *The Ecology of Human Development.* Cambridge, Mass.: Harvard University Press.

Children's Commisioner's Office and Revealing Reality, 2018, *Life in 'Likes'.* Available at: https://www.childrenscommissioner.gov.uk/publication/life-in-likes/ [Accessed 14.07.2018].

European Union, Regulation (EU) 2016/679 of the European Parliament and of the Council of 27 April 2016 on the Protection of Natural Persons with Regard to the Processing of Personal Data and on the Free Movement of Such Data, and Repealing Directive 95/46/EC (General Data Protection Regulation). Available at: https://eur-lex.europa.eu/legal-content/EN/TXT/PDF/?uri=CELEX:32016R0679 [Accessed 20.07.2018].

Great Britain, Department for Education, 2017, *Statutory Framework for the Early Years Foundation Stage.* Available at: https://www.gov.uk/government/publications/early-years-foundation-stage-framework--2 [Accessed 08.07.2018].

Great Britain, Standards and Testing Agency, 2017, *Early Years Foundation Stage Profile 2018 Handbook.* Available at: https://assets.publishing.service.gov.uk/government/uploads/system/uploads/attachment_data/file/669079/Early_years_foundation_stage_profile_2018_handbook.pdf [Accessed 14.07.2018].

Kinderly™, 2018. Available at: https://kinderly.co.uk/ [Accessed 20.07.2018].

Longfield, A., 2017, *Children's Commissioner Launches Social Media Giants' Terms and Conditions 'Jargon-buster' to Give Kids More Power in Digital World.* Available at: https://www.childrenscommissioner.gov.uk/2017/09/29/childrens-commissioner-launches-social-media-giants-terms-and-conditions-jargon-buster-to-give-kids-more-power-in-digital-world/ [Accessed 14.07.2018].

NSPCC, 2018, *Ten Years Since the Byron Review: Are Children Safer in a Digital World?* Available at: https://www.nspcc.org.uk/globalassets/documents/research-reports/byron-review-10-years-on-report.pdf [Accessed 08.07.2018].

Palaiologou, I., 2014, Children Under Five and Digital Technologies: Implications for Early Years Pedagogy. *European Early Childhood Education Research Journal*, 24 (1), 5–24

Piaget, J., 1936, *Origins of Intelligence in the Child.* London: Routledge & Kegan Paul.

Prensky, M., 2001, Digital Natives, Digital Immigrants Part 1. *On the Horizon*, 9 (5), 1–6.

Tapestry™, 2018. Available at: https://tapestry.info/ [Accessed 14.07.2018].

10 Conclusions

Moira Moran

In her introduction to this book, Kent proposes Bronfenbrenner's dynamic ecological systems theory as a structure for the approach adopted by the authors. This brief conclusion will review chapters in the light of some, though by no means all, aspects of that theory and specifically in relation to the development of children's communication.

Throughout the book the authors have reviewed aspects of communication for children in a wide sense: children's communications, communications with children, and communications about children. Communications have been considered which are verbal and non-verbal, spoken, written, and electronic. The views of those who communicate with and about children have been represented including the children themselves, parents and carers, practitioners, researchers, and elements of the wider community such as the media and producers of resources for children. In this respect the book has adopted the holistic approach of the title, presenting communication through the lens of interactions, relationships, and positive environmental contexts which can actively support a child's development.

When Bronfenbrenner in 1979 expounded his, then new, theoretical perspective of human development, he defined the theory of "ecology of human development" as one which focused on *"development-in-context"* (p. 13). He defined development as "a lasting change in the way in which a person perceives and deals with his environment" (p. 3).

In the same way as communication has been viewed holistically, as more than an aspect of learning and development in the EYFS, so development has been similarly viewed within the book. A holistic approach sees the whole as greater than the sum of its parts. Communication is a crucial and integral aspect of a child's development, and therefore a prime area in terms of the EYFS, but it is viewed throughout this book as more than that. Communication is seen as closely interwoven with and interdependent on all areas of development and best understood when considered as part of the whole. Within the chapters of the book multiple perspectives have integrated to provide optimal opportunities to interpret and support children's communication development. The important impact of personal, social, and physical environments on development have been recognised and discussed

Bronfenbrenner proposed that relationships with others facilitate children's development. He identified the "dyad" as "a critical context for development" and the "basic building block of the microsystem", explaining "a dyad is formed whenever two persons pay attention to or participate in one another's activities" (p. 56). This dyadic shared attention or participation defines a broad field of communication. Bronfenbrenner further stated that dyads can involve observation or joint activity, and, if strong, can continue to exist when both parties are not physically together: the "holding in mind" referred to by Ulanowsky in Chapter 2. He regarded reciprocal interactions within the mesosytem as situated in "strong and enduring emotional attachment" (p. 60) and as providing the best conditions for learning. Ulanowsky reviewed recent research to provide evidence for this hypothesis for the very youngest children, emphasising the two-person, reciprocal nature of the early interactions which support development of both parties.

In Chapter 3 Gripton explored a further element of the developmental dyad as identified by Bronfenbrenner: the shifting balance of power towards the developing person. Through her chapter which debated children's participation and perspectives, she advocated for a focus by the practitioner on attending to children's perspectives as a participatory process more empowering to the child within their microsystem than consultation on their voice. This power shift facilitates reciprocity and reflects the dynamic aspect of Bronfenbrenner's concept of development as "the person's evolving perception of the ecological environment, and his relation to it, as well as the person's growing capacity to discover, sustain or alter its properties" (p. 9). Therefore, in this chapter, Gripton invited us to consider how, in our practice, we can support children to become, in their turn, active participants with a valued voice and perspective in their microsystem and also in the wider circles in which they find themselves as they develop and grow.

Bronfenbrenner stated, "The capacity of a setting ... to function effectively as a context for development is seen to depend on the existence and nature of social interconnections between settings including joint participation, communication and the existence of information in each setting about the other" (pp. 5–6). He further defined the microsystem as "connections between other persons present in the setting, the nature of these links, and their indirect influence on the developing person through their effect on those who deal with him at first hand" (p. 8). Hobson and Farley (Chapter 4) exemplified good practice in their chapter's account of one setting's developmental project. The leadership's determination to engage on collaborative development involved each room (or setting within the whole nursery setting) participating jointly to share their expertise in the area of children's communication. The holistic approach is reported as resulting in a sum greater than all the parts, in the development of a communication-rich environment in which the community of practitioners are receptive to children's perspectives and support their developing communication skills.

In their research-based Chapter 5 Kent and McDonald further explored the part played by pedagogical leadership in the development of an effective environment for communication development. They identified the benefits, but also the challenges, of collaboration and communication within settings (microsytem) and between settings (mesosystem) to support provision and improvement of the enabling communication environment.

In the following three chapters of the book, authors turned their attention to aspects of the physical environment, to the extent to which the environment can enable and support communication, and to the messages that are communicated by the environment to and about children. Still within Bronfenbrenner's ecological system, the focus was on the role of a socially just approach to providing a communication and language-rich environment for all children where positive relationships are allowed to support children's developing sense of self and wellbeing.

Gripton in Chapter 6 addressed Bronfenbrenner's statement that "what matters for behaviours and development is the environment as it is *perceived* rather than as it may exist in 'objective' reality" (p. 4 Bronfenbrenner's punctuation), the way it is "experienced" (p. 22). Gripton presented the physical environment as, at its best, offering a communication bridge between child and adult supporting developmental dyads through play and participation. Gripton argued that in order for this bridge to be most effective for all children and adults, it should be constructed by child and practitioner collaboratively, again advocating for all children's active participation to facilitate their development. She also invited consideration of the overt and covert messages portrayed by the environment, and how these can be experienced by children and families, both individuals and groups.

Peart (Chapter 7) further developed the examination of the subtle messages communicated by the environment, through a specific discussion of the toys and resources offered to children within settings. Through her argument she explored the possible experiences and perceptions of children in settings which reflect only one image, one which does not necessarily reflect them, and she cast a light on Bronfenbrenner's observation: "within any culture or subculture, settings of a given kind – such as homes, streets, or offices – tend to be very much alike, whereas between cultures they are distinctly different" (p. 4). Thus, Peart again invited practitioners to reflect on the environment they provide and how it could be experienced by every child.

Bronfenbrenner described "The environmental events that are the most immediate and potent in affecting a person's development are activities that are engaged in by others with that person or in her presence" (p. 7). In Chapter 8 Moran took the environment of the outdoors as the context to exemplify such events. She proposed that the distinctive characteristics of outdoor experiences afford ample opportunities for developmental dyads involving joint activity, and that these can be sustained and in the power of the child, thus enabling "optimal conditions for learning and development" (p. 60). Her representation of the outdoor environment as an inclusive and neutral space supports its proposal as rich in potential for communication development.

Bronfenbrenner observed that the interconnections between settings "can be as decisive for development as events taking place within a given setting" (p. 3). In addition to the importance of the dyad for development, he identified the impact of the triad as equally important. The positive involvement of parents and carers, friends, and family in the child's community contribute significantly to the influence and effectiveness of the child and practitioner relationship in supporting potential development. He argues that when such connections are in place, effective and positive, their communications and interactions about the child have a crucial impact on the communications and interactions with the child. It is such communications concerning and about children between setting and home, or mesosytems, that were the subject of Cazaly's chapter (Chapter 9). She argued the importance of inclusive systems of communication that enable the contribution of all families and communities for their children.

While acknowledging the crucial value of communication between setting and home, Cazaly's chapter also touched on another aspect of Bronfenbrenner's theory: that of the macrosystem and "forces emanating from more remote regions in the larger physical and social milieu" (p. 13). She debated the recent developments in e-communications concerning the child and explored the unpredictable nature of the impact on the future child of these rapidly changing and developing systems.

Reference

Bronfenbrenner, U., 1979. *The Ecology of Human Development: Experiments by nature and design.* London: Harvard University Press.

Index

Page numbers in *italic* denote figures